The Age of Convergence

By Dan Ramsden

ISBN-13: 978-0615894683 (DreamTigerEquities)
ISBN-10: 0615894682
Library of Congress Control Number: 2013951439

"Knowledge is now fast becoming the sole factor of production, sidelining both capital and labor… Formal knowledge is seen as both the key personal and the key economic resource. In fact, knowledge is the only meaningful resource today."

Peter F. Drucker, *Post-Capitalist Society* (1993)

"From concentrated information come creatures of great beauty and complexity – indeed, of such complexity that sometimes the world's best mathematical minds cannot resolve it… In science, all important ideas need names and stories to fix them in the memory."

Benoit Mandelbrot, *The Misbehavior of Markets* (2004)

Contents

Second Part: Appendices & Notes

Products & Other Enticements

New Economies & Markets

New Labor & New Capital

The Digitized Character & Reorientation

Preface

1.

I began to jot down impressions on digital technology and the sector's evolution in late-2009 in a blog I called *Discourse and Notes*. This was approximately the time when Twitter was turning mainstream, and I continued this exercise with regularity through Twitter's IPO announcement. These milestones are worthy of consideration, the subject of this book considered.

As the name suggests, the blog was foremost my way of keeping notes and organizing my thoughts as I was studying. The financial crisis had just taken place, it was the time of policy and debate and some alarm, and Sequoia Capital had produced a set of warning slides that were making their way around the web, "Good Times RIP." It was a time when, in the technology ecosystem, several trends were developing in tandem: Traditional venture capital was on its way to consolidation, new forms of venture funding were emerging in seed finance (some think, to an eventual point of bubbling over), the startup community was growing fast (partly as a side-effect of seed funding growth, partly on the heels of a weak job environment, and partly in reflection of diminishing startup costs), and the largest technology incumbents were beginning to amass enormous cash troves.

Having been involved in finance and business strategy as a banker to the media and telecommunications sectors since the 1990s, I approached my study of new trends in digital technology with a historical eye, mindful of the stages that had led us to this point. And yet, there was something wholly unique and almost strange in the phenomena. This was an era of its own, I felt, and one that would some day be looked back upon with awe and reverence, like, say, the *industrial revolution* before. None of the commonly used names to reference what some thought was happening – *web*

2.0, or *mobile web*, or *social web* – captured the true bigness.

With this inherent preconception always in my mind, a conclusion drawn before the facts were gathered, I focused on and noted the continuations, similarities, and overlaps in a sector that was not technically "new" (as its occasional designation of "new media" implies) but rather an extension. And I sought to draw associations between the nature of new business models (and technologies) and their predecessors and counterparts in the segment.

Simultaneously, I also detected patterns taking shape in the capital markets and the funding structures that underpinned the modes of innovation and business building. These, too, like the underlying platforms that they sponsored and financed, while coming to resemble and extend from well-trodden fundamental terrain, began to manifest new patterns of their own, in public as well as private markets, which were increasingly like a mixture of new and old, equity and debt, individual and institutional. In short, a picture was coming into focus that seemed all the time more familiar despite its apparent novelty.

This was in the early and middle years within the timeframe in question, and it set the stage for subsequent developments and observations. I noticed a progression in the startup landscape that took media and technology companies in the direction of commerce and retail, which at least in my mind appeared like a new sub-segment, *transactional media*. And as *social media* grew and matured, I began to see an overlap between these connectivity platforms and their counterparts in other media subdivisions – *entertainment*, *information*, and again, *transactional*. While these observations gelled, a picture of general combination between the four spheres took shape, based on their respective anchor tenants and their constant movements towards each other: Facebook, Google, Amazon and Apple, at least symbolically, for there are many other samples. And this convergence continues.

But it didn't end there, and in fact, as it turns out, this was only an exemplary start, an early foundation. There was the emergence of new financial services and markets, which led to new forms of banking and capital flows and research, and which drew attention to the vagueness of the line between what is a media company and what is a financial institution. When Bloomberg acquired Business Week, when American Express began to dabble with Twitter and Foursquare, when LendingClub was formed with Wall Street sponsorship in Silicon Valley, the notion came home to roost. And I asked myself why the lines and differences were fading, why these convergences were happening, and where it would likely lead. The answer, increasingly, came down to information and the mechanization of knowledge.

This book is a summation of my analysis, containing a selection of essays on the subject first published in the *Discourse and Notes* blog. Although the mosaic has been organized by theme there is much overlap between the sections, as there is overlap in convergence itself. Both the mosaic form (rather than linear progression) and the overlap, thus, seem suited to the subject; and it might have been false, maybe even contrived, to present the material in any way other than as a mix of qualities and coincidental patterns.

Convergences – between media's four spheres, between media and commerce, media and finance, finance and commerce, hardware and software, technology and consumerism, early-stage and later-stage businesses, early-stage and later-stage capital, and several other blends – are recurring motifs in this book. And there is, as an overarching theme, the convergence of all of these into and around information and its processing. One might, indeed, step further back and look at the composite even more holistically, from where I believe the ultimate convergence will be visible. Although less obvious due to our own proximity, perhaps, it's a convergence that has likely been there all along: the balance and interplay of art and science.

2.

Before making a prediction it helps to understand the subject. Before drawing conclusions on a subject it helps to understand its context. The subject of an information age and its context requires purposeful attention. It is a new environment with a new set of rules and patterns. Although it may be recognized as such, it still remains for the most part guided, scrutinized, evaluated by classic filters, based on drivers and metrics rooted in classic models from a different time.

It isn't that these are not applicable in a new era, but their definitions and associations are different now, and to the extent these serve as guideposts for finance and economics – and branches that relate in technology, business, education, culture, and so many other extensions for that matter – then these guideposts have to be constantly visited and revisited and questioned.

The notes and commentaries in this book are an attempt to start such a process, and it is also an attempt to decompose the subject into pieces that might lend themselves to further scrutiny. The goal is not to make a forecast or promote a set of recipes, but maybe to take an inventory of items as a starting point.

From here, we can begin to formulate a view, a strategy, a structure...

3.

The narrative that follows is built on a core thesis, laid out in the first section and followed by related practical observations in the second. This core is augmented by footnotes and commentaries and caveats in the third and final part, which adds some depth and color to the surface discussion that precedes it. It isn't critical that these essays be read in order, but it won't hurt.

Thesis & Its Elements

1. Elementary particles

The elementary particles of a business, for purposes of this discussion, are the largely irreducible components that make up its core. These particles don't so much comprise forms of capital and labor, technology and systems, markets and locations, as the elements beneath the surface of those building blocks. These are the pieces that shape the structure, which shapes the enterprise.

In finance and markets, for instance, under the surface of capital flows and resources that drive these, are the analytics and decision-making. In commerce, before the eventual sales and advertising, are the supply chain investigation, market segmentation and targeting. In industry there is engineering and design and efficiency optimization. In healthcare there is research of both product and result.

What all these elementary particles share – and as is widely recognized as a defining feature in a knowledge-based economy – is that these are all information-centric. And what is becoming an increasingly common feature of information and its processing in our time, is that this is increasingly mechanized. Knowledge is thus decomposed into elementary particles in turn, and from there rebuilt.

By necessity of mechanization, the decomposition of knowledge into elementary particles that can be collected, packaged, analyzed, and distributed, creates a homogeneous texture that is data. The machine requires it, because the machine only understands instruction and formula, and this can only be communicated mathematically. That is a large-scale equalizer.

In other words, when elementary particles across a variety of fields are increasingly reduced to data and its processing, then these fields, on some level, are the same. If we define the elementary particles of a business, as we did for purposes of this discussion, as the largely irreducible components that make up its core, then fields that share similar elementary particles are essentially similar fields. This is a simplification.

It is a simplification because there is nuance and there is specialization, and knowledge is complex to say the least. It is a simplification because technology is not yet at the point where all manner of intricacy and subtlety that the human mind can comprehend is replicable by algorithm. But technology is heading that way and has made enormous strides.

As such technical progress continues, not only will essential differences between segments diminish (math and formula being transportable), but these fields will as a result lend themselves more readily to combination. We're noticing the beginning of such combinations in the growing overlap of media and commerce and finance and markets. And we will continue to see the phenomenon unfold – perhaps more deeply and more widely – in our era of convergence.

2. The language of industrial convergence

Industries can be defined by their language, on some level, even if there are differences of accent and dialect. Although there are aspects of language common to all business – for instance, the accounting language of profit and loss – this is akin to the fundamentals of grammar, the basic logic of which carries across variances of vocabulary and culture. To continue with this analogy, what sets industries apart is not the grammar but the terminology, expressions, definitions, the nouns and verbs and adjectives and grunts and other such symbols that collectively make up a bond, an understanding, and a shared system.

There may be familiarity in the translation, but on the surface the concept of, say, same-store sales in retail, would be an alien term to an oil exploration firm thinking about its equivalent idea in proven producing reserves, or a drug company thinking in terms of its patent portfolio. The translatability is not the point – as most words have their counterpart in most languages – but rather the ways in which traditional industries from commerce to energy to healthcare to finance, media, manufacturing, education, you name it, have been rooted in and also shaped by the terminology that mirrors value drivers.

Where I am going with this preamble is here: As information technology is adopted by all industry segments to a greater extent, the vocabulary of bits, analytics, storage, distribution, security, mobility, processing, integration, and so on, is creating a bridge between languages that were previously united only by accounting grammar. What's more, for many of the traditional sectors – notably finance, commerce and media – information processing and technology are becoming the core business itself, and we have reason to believe that other segments are following suit. (Note the industrial internet, robotics, and 3D printing as early trends in manufacture.)

When thus the grammar as well as the vocabulary itself start to blend across segments, and when this is a reflection of the deepening information (technology and processing) roots taking hold everywhere, the value drivers of previously disparate sectors begin to overlap. When value drivers overlap, there is little to actually separate one sector from another, and for all intents and purposes a convergence will have taken place. This is not a statement about causality or sequence, nor is it a prediction, it is rather an observation of certain realities with very real consequences that should be watched and understood.

The economic nature of information and its related technologies is particular, and the extent to which our standard economic models are ideally suited for an information economy is unclear. In debates about policy and its results, inflation and deflation, the increasingly pronounced divergence between economic performance and capital markets, even in debates about the qualities of economic study itself, unless this new context is specifically factored in, the argument on either side will have been incomplete, perhaps altogether misguided.

3. Creative integration as a new invention form

We often think about innovation and invention as synonymous, but strictly speaking this is incorrect. While technological invention is a sub-segment of innovation, the latter is a much broader field that includes a multitude of possibilities. The introduction of online coupons, for instance, was not any sort of invention – as coupons in a variety of forms had existed for a long time – but it was an innovative solution. It combined tried and tested methods in commerce with modern modes of delivery and processing, and the result was a new system.

When we now talk about disruption and technical progress, on a certain level we imply technological invention. Or at a minimum we imply innovative systems, such as the one described, based on the reinvention of older processes. There is another form of innovation, however, which may become a more prevailing theme ahead, and this is the combination and integration of previously disparate pieces in new ways. The acquisition of Buddy Media by Salesforce.com would be an innovative move, as is the combination of Oracle and Vitrue. (Facebook's purchase of Instagram (which is not a technically inventive platform) is a newly integrated feature for subscribers and a new mobile opportunity for the acquirer. That is innovation, too, in its own way, if we step back and think about it fairly.)

In the cited instances of combinational innovation, the merging has been between disparate pieces that are nevertheless within a shared sphere of influence. The even more interesting combinations, however, are in the overlap of previously disparate spheres. The convergence of media and commerce has been manifested in transactional media, with Amazon, Ebay and Groupon leading the charge. The convergence of media and finance is picking up momentum all the time. Bloomberg (media company or financial markets platform?) is the most visible symbol of this combination, but we also look to Square and Kickstarter and Lending Club for inspiration and example.

Next in line, even if perhaps slow on the uptake, are traditional media and their potential convergence with all of the above. In our collective enthusiasm for new stuff, we have been quick to dismiss the older media and write these off for their absence of modernity. But there is value – maybe still unrealized – in the massive audiences and brands, and we shouldn't assume that these assets can only be monetized in the traditional ways. Just as the combinations of media and commerce, media and finance, social and transactional, have brought on innovative modes, so too the combination of traditional media with modern systems might give rise to new possibilities.

This is our new and massive innovation wave: it is *creative integration*. And thus the optimal dimensions for operators, investors, entrepreneurs, and their advisors, must include a greater than ever element of multi-disciplinary understanding. In addition to deep analysis, an ability to synthesize disparate elements into a cohesive whole will be imperative. Specialization is important, but adaptation more so. And flexibility, rather than insular enforcement, will rule the roost.

4. "Connected systems"

A guy said: "To bear a name is to claim an exact mode of collapse." Cioran was a cranky old cat, to be sure, and most of the time he was yanking chains. In jest, though, there is some truth, and jesters can be as truthful as anyone. The quotation may be applied to many things, one of which is the weight and limiting rigidity of solid objects in an environment that's been and always will be fluid. It is vaguely about what Dr. Taleb would refer to as robustness, as distinct from fragility and "antifragility." The latter, according to the author, gains from disorder, the former two do not. In an environment marked by change, by disorder, optionality gains and solid objects don't. The idea of names and their firmness somehow relates to strategy and direction.

A business name, like the title of a book, is a core feature of the enterprise. It reflects the underlying asset, the culture, the origins, and might at times predict (or better still, determine) the outcome. Much like the title of a book might directly or indirectly hint at its conclusion, so too the name of a business – like DNA – carries a portion of its fate. A name can define a product, or the product may give substance to the name. The interplay is the thing – each transformed by and containing the other – where the name is both seed and packaging.

One of the more inspired strokes, perhaps to no surprise, has been the naming of *Apple Computer*. In the context of a dynamic and evolving environment that is one day hardware, the next media, then commerce, and really all of these together, a technical name would have been restricting, and a cute fluffy name would have cheapened the experience of an artful product. *Apple* – and we can each of us interpret the word and symbol in any multitude of ways, from nature to Newton to the Book of Genesis – now also has a new significance in the popular lexicon.

But strokes are not always inspired, while naming is necessary not only in persons and entities. Industry segments, for example, must also be called this or that, and the selection is prone to work in sometimes unknown ways. In a market increasingly dominated by Pandora and Spotify and streaming services, what does the name *Radio* actually mean? Where does the line get drawn between an exchange and, say, AngelList, which is presumably a social network? As fleeting as names and definitions are, as vulnerable to obsolescence, backfire, or malfunction, they are essential to crystallizing thoughts and staking a claim to an existence. Radio had to be called something, but maybe it's wrong to call Pandora that.

In the assortment of segments in this book, the subject of convergence is dealt with at some length and in a large variety of ways. Although I am mindful of what pitfalls there are in naming things, it is important, I think, to give the converging catalog a name. I like *connected systems*: the convergence of distinct segments into and around information technology and processes. Although the idea and name, both, may one day be obsolete, I think we need to recognize the phenomenon in the present case. Product builders and strategists need to understand that the industry they're in is no longer, say, Radio, or even *financial markets*, but something that takes part of a bigger integrated whole, centered around bits and flows.

Taleb, options trader, says: "We know more than we think we do, a lot more than we can articulate." The statement opens a chapter called "On the Necessity of Naming."

5. Capital, markets and knowledge exchanges

Information flow is a slippery subject. Pinning down information and its meanings is as difficult sometimes as determining the correct placement of the line between symmetry and asymmetry. These are complex and heady debates, and where years might be spent in chatter and Nobel Prizes, markets tend to settle issues more gracefully. This is why we love markets so very dearly, among other reasons: There is brevity and insight in markets that are as elegant as any minimalist design.

But even if markets in whole are thus, the quality is based on an aggregation of points of uneven uniformity. An analogy could be drawn to a large ensemble – thousands of voices in unison, creating harmonies and effects – reduced to grotesquery when the singing stops but for a handful of tone-deaf enthusiasts who have not yet finished with their notes. The underlying mess exposed, we have to reconsider the music. But we shouldn't, because the performance was complete and unified enough. So too with markets, even when they appear to break.

Whether wholesome or broken, artificial or natural (and where anyway can one draw that line?), liquid or not, markets are voices that teach lessons, if we would listen, and sometimes we hear a message that we inherently already know:

Capital and information follow one another in harmony, and both tend to flow to where the stream runs deepest.

If recent convergences, as described, are highlighting any one thing especially, it may be that in the duality of capital and knowledge it is the latter, more than the former, that leads. So it follows, then, that capital markets are and have always been sub-segments of media, or, more particularly speaking, of information and its processes. This is a point to which we will frequently return:

The future bank will be a media conglomerate, in fact already is.

6. Post-capitalist economics

From sector elements thus framed, we can consider the broader economy, defined by its connected systems and knowledge base. In the term knowledge one can infer many things, and for the present case let's include all and any. Technologists will instantly think of data and its assorted flows and designs, and there is that. But there is also education and medicine and law and finance and other services, there is news and reporting and research, there are the many branches of science, there is even entertainment, with its own special knowledge. A cab driver's knowledge is critical to the cab driver's job, as is a chef's, as is an engineer's. The type and complexity of knowledge may vary, and also the skill of the knowledge worker, but ownership of knowledge is a common link to all these areas.

In a knowledge-based economy of connected systems, the value unit is information. It is important to understand this and to understand its implications. Not to suggest that information was ever not valuable, it always has been, but in an economy dominated by knowledge-work, information becomes the medium of exchange and, in ways, the very currency. What's more, information and knowledge is now increasingly (and with greater sophistication) digitized and converted to manageable bits. Which can be automated and mechanically transferred.

The terms currency and exchange are being thrown around here in the context of knowledge and information and bits purposefully. Because these are economic terms that are the root of economic science, while knowledge and information and bits are increasingly the drivers of economies in a time when physical transport plays a less dominant role than the transport of data.

Peter Drucker predicted a *Post-Capitalist Society*, in which knowledge-work is the dominant driver, and it seems he was right. By extension, a post-capitalist economics would be a science to explain and formulate the production, distribution, and consumption of goods and services in the context of knowledge and information as core value units. Ideas such as inflation and deflation, for instance, will have special characteristics in the case of information. The more fundamental concept of supply and demand comes with a special set of quirks when knowledge is the subject. Monetary policy, based as it is on currency as the store of value, may be understood differently, or more comprehensively, were currency and value reassessed in this new context. Fiscal policy, used as it is to supplement and direct business and social activity, might refocus on a new set of relevant targets.

In a knowledge economy based on connected systems, the study of economics is itself no longer a detached framework of observation but a subject. As economists might study widget manufacturing and medicine and law and cab driving from an angle that the respective practitioners may be too close to see, so also economics may benefit now from an outside and more removed perspective. It's just one more example on the list, another service provider and advisor to advisors to advisors.

7. Towards a new economics, cont'd

If there were a company that hoarded cash while borrowing money at almost no cost, that launched new products to offer more features for the same or a lesser price (and these products made more and more "free stuff" possible), all things being equal, one would say this company was showing many characteristics we'd associate with a deflationary system. When we further observe that some customers might skip new product versions knowing that another, before long, will be economically more attractive, we would conclude that these customers are behaving in a way characteristic of deflationary psychology. These are examples.

This passage isn't about a company or a customer segment. It is about economic signals and patterns, recognizing, or at least suspecting, that economics is not even really a science, let alone an imperfect one, and that its "laws" are merely markers in an ocean. Matters of yes and no are rare in this field, where almost all matters are about more or less, and sometimes about finding pieces of vague puzzles that may or may not fit its always changing picture. This, at least, is what I have observed, and I have only observed some things.

The other day I observed an interesting debate (free of charge online) between two prominent venture investors. One argued that technology innovation has slowed while the other argued the contrary. When asked for hard evidence to support their otherwise anecdotal positions, the latter pointed to the surge in advanced technical and scientific degrees at universities, while the former pointed to falling market valuations of technology companies in the past ten years (after stripping out a handful of the very dominant players from the aggregate). Both acknowledged the flaws in their measurement systems, but what else is new, this is economics, and a proxy for science is better than no science at all.

Now, it's quite conceivable that both of them are right. Because it's possible for innovation to increase and its financial value to simultaneously fall, in the aggregate, if one presupposes a deflationary rather than inflationary environment. Coming out of an extended era of Edison and Ford and IBM and Intel and Hewlett-Packard and Apple, we tend to equate technical innovation with economic wealth creation; but what if the data presented by the opposing sides in the referenced debate in fact leads to a different set of circumstances and new context?

When entrepreneurial theorists advise founders to raise cash when they can get it, that is consciously or unconsciously deflationary advice: All things equal, in a deflationary economy cash is more valuable than equity. When entrepreneurs sell their businesses in so-called "acquihires," or otherwise plan for early exits at a theoretical fraction of what these businesses may have been worth if they had stuck it out for a few more years, these are consciously or unconsciously deflationary decisions. When we note that it's cheaper than ever to launch a technology business, for a variety of well-known reasons, that's a deflationary observation.

These subjects are obviously more nuanced than presented, and very complex. The perspective highlighted is one angle among many, and like any angle in the economic realm it is relative rather than absolute. Nevertheless, it's an angle worthy of consideration and may in its small part explain broader economic experience – for instance, that general inflation rates have been historically and almost unnaturally low at the time of this writing, despite enormous liquidity infused by central banks worldwide.

In the previous chapter the possibility was broached about a new economic investigation and new analytic method to reflect a changing economic landscape in which information and knowledge are new drivers of capital formation. Should such a new study emerge, it will be as fickle as its predecessors, but like its predecessors it will serve its purpose of demarcation and guideline... Until it, too, like its predecessors, runs its course and is succeeded.

8. Energy and information

Supply and demand. Regardless of item, geography, time or circumstance, the fundamental equation has withstood it all and likely always will. Economists will debate variations, derivatives, causalities, outcomes and so on, but the basis isn't questioned. The value of financial instruments grows or diminishes based on supply and demand, even if this follows a trend or future expectation. The value of goods and services, similarly; and so too capital and labor and interest rates and all the things that interconnect and cause and result. It's a messy business, but *supply and demand*, as an idea and steadfast mathematics, stays clean.

Sometimes we see bonds and stocks and other stores of value behave in a certain fashion on account of certain statements that are made by a certain authoritative source of both supply and demand. Certain questions are raised about economic trends and outcomes, certain interpretations are made, perhaps about inflation and employment, interrelated and complex, difficult to measure with precision. The ensuing tumult reflects supply and demand confusion, if you will, on several economic levels, leading to financial market imbalances.

As this takes place, in another part of the world an industrial event is happening. A technical demonstration is on display, involving electricity and efficient transport, solar power and information technology. Tesla's presentation is in purposeful contrast to the older-world manner of oil and the more analog system of filling stations. On one hand, a precise and almost sterile solution directly or indirectly predicated on bits and circuitry, on the other hand a mechanism rooted in physical boundaries, natural constraints and, as it were, dirty hands. There is symbolism in this event, running parallel with market volatility.

The overlay – and the preceding has all been based on a true story – speaks to a major transition. It speaks to a transformation that started with large-scale energy and energy solutions and is leading to an information efficiency that may soon replace these as the gravitational core. There is a transition underway that may be characterized as a changing of the guards from an energy economy to an information economy. The consequences will be as intricate as the underlying supply and demand variables, particularly as information and its technological aspects follow principles that are markedly different from what we have been accustomed to in the industrial complex heretofore.

Whether taken literally or symbolically, an energy economy is based on the extraction, production, distribution and consumption of finite resources, in which labor (a limited pool) features prominently. The supply and demand equation in such a context is confined to fixed and known variables. In contrast, an economy driven by information technology is characterized by an effectively infinite supply of bits and the arguably limitless possibilities of mechanized invention. When the supply side is opened up in this fashion, the demand side requires adaptation for sustainable economic balance to form. This, in the last analysis, may be the true fundamental undercurrent we are witnessing, and it is a transition perhaps beyond the scope of policy and its pulls and strings.

9. Perpetuity and finality in disrupted settings

Finality and perpetuity play a central role in finance. The valuation of an asset presupposes one of the two, and from here other financial qualities follow – a need, a structure, access, etc. When the concept of finality is introduced, the asset is by definition a depleting asset. That is to say, the passage of time diminishes its value. Contrariwise, when an asset is deemed perpetual, its value is not only sustained but may even grow with variances that will emerge. These are all oversimplifications to introduce a further discussion, which isn't about discrete assets but business evaluation in an era of connected systems.

When an investment is made in a business, it is generally on the basis that the business is an ongoing concern and that its worth can be estimated, rightly or wrongly, as the present value of its future economic production. This future doesn't only include an income (or loss) stream, but also a terminal value. That is an arbitrary figure established at an arbitrary point in time, when it is assumed that ownership of the business is transferred from one investor to another. The concept of a terminal value partly supposes a finite holding period by one investor, but it is also a way to summarize the future without having to forecast profits and losses forever.

This terminal, in other words, is a way to condense the subsequent forecast into its own present value, if you will, at some future point. It is an endless cycle. One investor today estimates the value of a business according to what some future investor might pay. This future investor is a projection, a specter, who will in turn base his or her estimation on what some even more remote phantom will at some remoter point think; and so on, and so on, and so on…

An interesting practical phenomenon of these considerations is the following: In an ongoing concern, the present value of the business is very substantially (sometimes entirely) determined by the described terminal value, whereas the interim profits (or losses) represent a small (sometimes negligible) component. In other words, when an investment is made or when a business is acquired, there is often an implicit acknowledgment of perpetuity, and this determines the value of the business in a not insubstantial way. Were an investor or acquirer to see the target as finite, in contrast, the amount he or she would agree to pay would be limited to the remaining (and probably diminishing) income stream.

The discussion so far has been general enough that it might apply to any field and any business form. But we are in particular focused on information, media, and related technologies. In this field we run into external business influences such as consumer tastes that develop or change, technology obsolescence and innovation, and combinations and permutations of all of that. Perpetuity in such a field is a pretty strong word. We need only think of typewriters, pagers, increasingly now printers and newspapers, soon enough perhaps desktop computers, hard-drives, scheduled television programs, recorded music in general, to say nothing of credit card transactions and point-of-sale terminals.

The thought that occurs is not so much about finality and asset depletion – although in some cases that thought may be fitting – as it is about renewal and reinvention that must always take place in order for perpetuity to be justified. And perpetuity must be justified in order for certain valuations to make sense.

10. Business models and options: a synopsis

From these macro-economic elements loosely framed, we can reconsider micro-elements. We can evaluate business building in information-based enterprise (connected systems) with a fresh look. Even if there is no prescribed formula or clear-cut response for every challenge, we can at least revisit some of the accepted norms and explanations. We may in some cases even reassess old conclusions that were drawn.

For instance, there is the universally accepted precept of a business model. In the traditional sense this is determined by ways of building revenue and profit. It is in essence a framework in which the income and cash flows statements serve as guideposts. Perhaps the emphasis on these two financial statements was born from practical budgeting realities, and maybe our conventional business valuation method of *discounted cash flows* has reinforced this way of thinking. It is a system, however, that is rooted in an era when industries and businesses were believed to be more or less perpetual in nature, and when growth was aided by varying degrees of inflation. The first point has been proven flawed, at least in technology (and this is extending its branches everywhere), while the second point has at best also weakened (and mostly vanished).

But even then, and as described in the prior chapter, even in the traditional mode the result of discounted cash flows valuation is composed quite substantially – in many cases entirely – from a terminal value rather than the interim profits of the enterprise to that point. This terminal value concept presupposes a willing future buyer for the business, who will acquire it at a certain price. At that point in time, this buyer will in theory also conduct a discounted cash flows evaluation, directly or indirectly, that will similarly be based on a willing buyer even later in the same way. And so on, and so on, as has already been said. Considering the pace of change and reinvention that takes place in information technology (which, as stated, is extending its branches everywhere), it is impossible – or at least exceedingly difficult – to think of any terminal value with confidence, outside of a very heavy dose of *optionality*. (By optionality we refer to future possibilities that are not currently contemplated, that can't with precision be assessed, that are made possible by an existing asset that is owned. The value of an option increases with volatility in a given environment.)

Returning now to the idea of business models and revenues, if the task is to build enterprise value or to evaluate it, a business model has merit mainly to the extent that it does not diminish optionality, and ideally enhances it. The merit of revenue exists mainly to the extent that it is a cheaper source of funding than outside capital. These qualities all go hand in hand and are part of a cause-and-effect chain that is almost circular in nature. Out of these complexities, moreover, some key considerations emerge in our current era of connected systems:

(1) The option value of a product can diminish with time, unless upgraded or refreshed. (2) The absence of a business model can be stretched for so long before optionality benefits are no longer a sufficient offset. (3) Along the spectrum of information-based enterprise, technology at one extreme has shorter life and briefer option exercise potential than networks, which are harder to replace at the other end. (4) Many businesses fall in a zone between the polar extremes, or combine elements of both that need to be considered on a blended basis accordingly. (5) The timing decision of investments and exits is as important financially as the building or buying of a new business is strategically. (6) A focus on revenues is strictly speaking necessary for a business that seeks to stay independent, but not all businesses seek that or should do so, even if some might pretend for tactical reasons. (7) Some businesses are good at making money, and some are not; the former is not necessarily superior to the latter, nor more valuable, but each may want to pursue the other as partner.

11. A lens for evaluating the bits

We start small and work our way outward. At the core there is the value unit, which isn't the bit but what its batches stand for. We may call this *information*, but it includes a great deal besides. In the sense of media there is *content*. In finance and commerce there is *data*. There is *knowledge* more broadly, related to knowledge work, in science, education, law, and so on; in all services. Increasingly information (via bits) is integrated with production of goods. The list goes on, and its categories tend to overlap. So for simplicity we may generally call the items information, and regard this core as the value unit.

This is a depleting asset when left alone, because it has life only as information is relevant. Data, news, behavior changes, are information that might only be momentary. Some information has much longer shelf-life, especially if we include arts and entertainment. But even then it's a matter of degree, perhaps even in the sciences. Supply and demand factor in and complicate calculations, but when dealing with information we're dealing with perpetual supply, almost by definition, and some knowledge is more quickly set aside than another. For purposes of this discussion though, we should limit ourselves to information that's shared in bits (in the age of mechanical reproduction). A depleting asset.

This value unit, however, is processed through systems. (We refer here again to the connected systems that are the general category of our investigation.) These serve to renew, replenish, refresh, the life and thus the value of information, more or less effectively as different information lends itself to such processing more or less readily. Information systems, in the technical sense of bits and bit flows, have largely tended to be deflationary in nature. Moore's Law, open-source, web distribution, shared storage, and other such efficiency features of digital technology contribute to a lowering of barriers and business costs, and to a set of consumer expectations predicated on "free" or, at the very least, lower prices over time.

In this environment of a depleting value unit processed through deflationary systems, platforms exist to create enterprise value. They do so in a variety of ways that includes technology upkeep and improvement, feature integration, economies of scale, security, network effect, brand presence, and related staples of the digital media and information technology segments – which are increasingly converging with counterparts in finance, commerce, education, healthcare, hardware, and others, as has been noted. The link, once again, is information and its qualities and flows. It is the common language, in a sense, and enterprise value created through it very much depends on its fluency and economics.

Enterprise value consists of two basic ingredients: a core business asset and its optionality. The former is the foundation, the actuality, and the latter is its future possibilities, many of which unknown. The value of a platform is determined not only by the success with which it currently operates, but by its ability to do so with equal or greater success ahead. For an enterprise to grow into and justify its option value, in the context of the information environment described, it must continuously fine-tune its platform and reload its systems. In the financial sense, this equates to long-term life (perpetuity), and an ongoing stream of willing buyers for its product (even as it may be reinvented), and for itself.

The balance between the core asset and the optionality varies with different types of platforms and different stages in the enterprise cycle. At one extreme, the pure startup, the value proposition is likely all option based. At the other extreme, say, the mature utility, the option value will be very low. In between these two ends is where most financial activity takes place, and structures are determined by the blend of optionality on the upside and asset coverage on the downside. In an information-based environment – characterized by economic drivers and market profiles as described in the preceding pages – financing structure and business valuation take on special features that reflect it.

... Or at least, they should. And the nuances of venture capital, later-stage lower-risk equity, debt funding in its many manifestations, the differences between liquid and illiquid positions, strategic versus purely financial investment, and the timing of investment exits, all should be understood in the depicted context of bits, value units, systems, and platforms... even as financial asset classes themselves converge and take on characteristics of the underlying sectors they target and support.

This chapter is dense and may be worth re-reading (although I would not presume), because through this entry all the preceding and upcoming passages connect.

12. Concluding and summarizing the argument

There is a convergence underway driven by information technology. Whole industry segments are adapting to systems based on bits and the processing of these to transform in ways that range from the superficiality of branding and messaging all the way into the very fundamental core of products and how business is conducted. In varying degrees, this is taking place in finance and markets, commerce, education, healthcare, obviously media (as much an enabler as a target in this trend), automobiles and transport, and even the manufacture of goods, light and heavy.

Examples are too numerous to mention, and the pattern is so pronounced that it seems superfluous to point to the evolution of 3-D printing, self-driving cars, the internet of things, or information-based currencies. It might almost be passé at this stage to bring up crowdfunding, programmatic advertising, the quantified self, let alone electronic commerce, high-frequency trading, open courseware, or artificial intelligence. To speak of "the cloud" and various XaaS offerings is as fascinating now as to refer to such ancient novelties as the worldwide web. In short, much of the preceding may be stating the obvious.

Where from here is the more interesting question, and at the top of this article the idea was repeated about convergences that are taking place. As touched upon in previous chapters, this is manifest in the combination of disparate sectors – such as, for instance, the combination of social media and finance in the fields of research, capital markets, and payment solutions – and I have argued that all of the industry categories referenced to this point are converging with information technology itself. The distinction between the use of this as a tool and an actual convergence with the very segment is not insignificant. It implies a merger, as it were, rather than an acquisition; or, stated differently, an adoption of each side by the other.

This is a critical aspect of a central thesis. When information – broadly defined as anything that can be transferred in bits – and its collection, processing, safekeeping, packaging, and distribution, serve as a common partner with multiple industry segments, then information technology as a sector in its own right takes on a dominant economic role. And then it isn't only that finance, commerce, education, transport, manufacture, and so on, are converging with but almost rather *into* information technology. In other words, this is not just a tool to facilitate enterprise but is the core business itself, and at some point in time the various industry categories may become sub-segments under the large overarching cover.

The point is not merely academic, and even if the perspective proves to be exaggerated in coming years this will be mainly a matter of degree. The trends described are happening, not futuristically dreamt up, and the underlying thesis therefore is a lens and clarifying filter with immediate ramifications. In the future, perhaps not very distant, the most dominant industrial platforms will be at the center of the information flow. Value creation will then be marked by different characteristics from those in an economy more rigidly capital- and labor-intensive, and less digitally awash in processed bits and their connected systems.

Words of Encouragement & Caution

1. Why and how convergence matters

If thus far the subject of discourse has been the convergence of previously disparate segments into and around information technology, processing, and media, it is also about the emerging overlap of different financial asset classes and structures. This mirrors an economy that seems perpetually in a state between origin and maturation, always on its way, never arrived.

Such considerations aren't trivial for investors or entrepreneurs – and on some level everyone fits into one of these two baskets, maybe both, at times – and here is why. For business builders there is the growing possibility that their competitors won't in a year or two be the same competition they face today, or that they expect to face. This isn't just a matter of company specifics, but whole sectors as these increasingly encroach on one another's terrain. Media, commerce, finance, technology: where can we now draw a rigid line between them? Hardware, software, information, connectivity, design: where does the integration fall apart? Early-stage venture, mature business: Which category does Twitter fit into?

Such rhetorical questions, in turn, are mirrored in finance that supports activity. Funding solutions and alternatives – venture capital, growth equity, debt, M&A – are overlapping and more often observed in parallel (rather than sequential) patterns.

For investors the issue is one of analysis and liquidity, and it relates directly to the same themes. The question is one of risk assessment and valuation in a context that is less formulaic all the time. In an environment in which media, technology, commerce, finance, hardware, services, and various capital markets float in a homogeneous mix, the nature of investment exit is apt to deviate from the more classical traditions. The strategic takeout at a future point is thus less predictable, or will, perhaps, be driven by a new formula in time.

It could be the social media giant or it could be the credit card company. It could be the bank, the retailer, or the hedge fund. It could be an alternative quasi-public offering in a new market, or it could be a recapitalization deal using leverage. Coming out of an environment of silos – an industrial complex defined by goods, materials, and rigid definitions of capital and labor – in short, an environment populated by assets, we readapt now, as we must, to an environment of options.

2. The evidence and news to watch

In sector news lately, you can see evidence mounting if you would watch it from the suggested perspective. You can see the crossroads and the intersection, the signposts marking its arrival. Somewhere before maturation but well along to that elusive point, the profile of a crossroads will continue thus a while. Here are some signals from along the way:

A hedge fund pestered Apple, no longer innovating rapidly enough it seems, to release its hoard of cash to shareholders, who could perhaps think of other uses. The structure offered to facilitate this transference was the creation of a new class of senior securities that are not quite debt obligations but a step in that direction. Debt, in my mind, hints at maturation, while equity hints at untapped possibility. A structure that is not pure debt and not pure equity, hints at a state of transition.

Speaking of debt obligations and transition, Dell wants to complete a leveraged recap to go private. It also wants to tap into cash stockpiles to augment this financial engineering. This is to say, Dell wants to use cash that might have been for the other kind of engineering instead.

Financial engineering often begins when the other kind diminishes, but not necessarily, not always. But sometimes, at a crossroads.

Leaving the referenced markers to the side for the time being, here are some other signals from a different direction. At Google there has been innovative talk of self-driving cars, new mobile advertising mechanisms, personalized search algorithms; but also, on the other hand, old-fashioned fiber networks and spectrum acquisition. At Facebook there is a new search engine. As Amazon works on text-to-speech conversion, it is also offering data hosting and free shipping. The directions, you see, become more scattered as we wander towards the intersection, and signals point to overlap and branches and commoditization, even as we make our way through the novelty.

Which really is the essence of a crossroads. It's a junction where extremes are replaced by means and middles, where contrast is supplanted with overlap. It is a place where traffic moves from and into multiple directions, and where congestion happens. At this juncture there has been all of that. There is overlap by segment, capitalization structure, asset class, and business stage. There is convergence of strategic and financial interest. There is a growing union of goal, even if from assorted angles. And the lanes in and lanes out are more than likely merging. In due course, but surely.

The time of newspapers on one hand, and, on the other, some novelty bird-app for micro-messaging, is gone. These are both media projects now. The time of premium devices and Windows software is past. These are becoming commodities and blending into one. Pure venture capital is getting scarcer, and venture funds are chasing later stages. Hedge funds are buying private shares, and corporations are targeting the upstarts.

The common thread and a recurring message, regardless of the angle, is what I believe to be – in this environment especially – the value of universality and openness. I am referring to that which is opposed to insularity. I argue against defensive status quo, and for adaptive commerce. To wrap up this commentary, therefore, I conclude as follows:

Through a busy intersection the safest approach is with the flow of traffic.

3. Distinctions in transactional complexity

The subject previously was finance, even if strategically presented. The discussion was mainly about asset classes and funding structures in an environment in mid-life, way past birth though not quite at maturity. Between these symbolic bookends – with venture finance symbolically on one side and mature capital (buyout and late-stage private equity) at the other – a transitional mix seems to be in formation, containing some elements of both in combination. This was an implied and otherwise explicit theme in the prior chapter, in the context of industry groups also in flux, approaching one another.

The current topic, continuing along similar themes, is mergers and acquisitions. The two subjects (finance and M&A) are related and are in ways extensions of themselves. Venture and other private equity financings often lead to acquisition, while acquisitions often require finance. But where funding is in large part a structural exercise, acquisitions are strategic. And here also the distinction between a new technology, new service, new business model, on one hand, and a mature asset type on the other, makes a difference in the nature of the transaction, its underlying strategy, and manner in which the deal is executed.

When media as a category was mature, say in the mid-90s, there was a great deal of consolidation between properties that were generally standardized in their profile. Market coverage (geographical, demographic, or possibly both) may have been contiguous or not, market sizes and market share may have varied, operations were more or less profitable, but the nature of the underlying business was easy to define, communicate, and understand. In the traditional media segments this is largely still true now, and when dealing in the exchange and trade of such mature properties within like categories, the M&A activity is also standardized.

The strategic decision in such instances is principally one of core expansion, eliminating a competitor, or value chain integration. It isn't a simple decision, but it follows a fairly formulaic path once it is made. It is supported by precedent and financing availability – if the price is right and the market is cooperative and so on (which is not always the case) – and the universe of transactors is established and relatively stable. Processes are often conducted through an organized auction, and it is appropriate to do so given the nature of the asset and the target segment.

When a technology is in its infancy, however, formula goes out the window. When customer habits and adoption are in transition, and when business models are still moving targets, acquisition strategies (and by extension sale processes) are a new undertaking each time. There is little rule of thumb and the idea of an auction process is less likely to fit the bill. In these instances there is explaining to do, strategic redirection to consider, the integration of novelty into established order, and the roadmap can be fuzzy, both ahead and behind. In the newer media universe and its ecosystem of technologies, this has, broadly speaking, or often enough, been the case.

Given the point at which the sector now finds itself – a point somewhere between birth and adulthood, where several disparate subgroups are combining, as wholly separate industries are adopting modes that bring them into a new digital information fold – this transactional state of affairs will not only continue but possibly become more pronounced. Not only are strategies becoming more complex because the field is more crowded and overlapping, but the margins for error are lesser. For the same reason.

4. New finance and the lost art of match-funding

All the innovation in the world doesn't change fundamental corporate finance. We may not value some assets the way we once did, we may not always have revenue to compare or cash flow to multiply, but assets are still governed by asset rules. We just have to look at it that way, which is to say, we have to remember that we are dealing with assets. For instance, assets have fixed lives – it's only a question of how soon – and between now and then assets depreciate, amortize, or deplete. Further, assets are funded with liabilities, and it is best for the two sides to overlap. Back in the day when corporate finance precepts were based on a greater vocabulary than Series A and IPO, there was the notion of match-funding. This had to do with the term of liabilities (not to be taken literally as debt only, but any financing) as corresponding with the life of a given asset. The two went hand in hand back then, and theoretically still do. We only have to look at it that way.

To take these old-fashioned concepts from the era of leveraged buyouts and inventory cycles and working capital management to the new one of innovation and venture rounds, we should begin by thinking of apps and technology solutions and websites as the new inventory and working capital and so on. Like inventory, like property and plant and equipment, like accounts receivable, the new apps and sites and technology solutions are assets with finite lives. For instance: the mainframe, the disk, or the Walkman, or for that matter the physical book, the TV network, the web portal. In some cases the asset manager, as it were, has been able to reinvent or introduce new assets – IBM being an example – and in other cases this is less so.

From this synopsis, which is limited although extensive enough to get us going, we derive several themes: Different types of technology solutions and apps and sites have different (expected) lives; some owners and operators are able to extend the lives of some assets, and others are not; some owners and operators manage a better portfolio than others, knowing how (and when) to acquire, exit, reinvent, or transform; and the match-funding of assets is, at least theoretically, based on a fluid equity profile that is as long- or short-lived as a given asset or asset portfolio warrants. Between these ideals and the reality of frenzied innovation, funded privately and not necessarily efficiently, there is one general disconnect that is worth noting.

On one hand: Entrepreneurs and their funding sources alike often talk about differences between products, features and businesses, but not so much about life expectancy. In this regard, there are substantial differences in profile. Some technologies – security software, for example, which gets hacked or otherwise rendered old fairly quickly – might have a limited term to maturity, as it were, while a network asset is likely to linger around and sustain repeated beatings. It isn't that these networks will survive into perpetuity – we see now that cable systems are even at risk of cord cutting – but there is a resilience to networks that mere technologies just don't enjoy. And in between, there are variations, permutations, and combinations, which can cause (expected) lives to vary along a continuum.

On the other side of the ledger: At least in the early stages of development – from birth to infancy and into adolescence at the very least – the funding of these assets is, as a rule, uniform in term. The sequence is usually one of seed finance to a variety of venture capital series, all (or most) of which are private and marked by uneven liquidity options. Institutional participants in these financings typically strive for five- to ten-year capital commitments, and this is a general rule of (financial) asset-class that doesn't seem to differentiate between varying (operating) asset-life profiles, as noted.

In short, the idea of match-funding may be lagging in a financial system that is based on fixed structures and limited flexibility.

A fair amount has been written about sub-standard returns in venture capital in the 2000's era, especially as the effect of the late-90's bubble has been processed out of the ten-year calculation. The discussion has for the most part honed in on issues of amount and an excess of capital supply. Correctly, this is an angle driven by ever-diminishing startup costs in the technology segment. But in the past decade another phenomenon has emerged, which is a quickening of maturation cycles for these businesses. It is no longer standard fare that maturation is a multi-year process, and by extension neither is life-expectancy insulated by such a cushion.

As life terms have been exposed, in a manner of speaking, and are now a purer function of technology type, as discussed, we might begin to see the funding decision also evolve. It isn't clear that the startup ecosystem is as advanced in this regard as its more mature corporate finance counterparts, but the basic tenets of corporate finance apply to startups as much as mature companies – especially so in an environment in which the distinction between one and the other is blurry at best, and arbitrary at least.

Not all early-stage businesses are equally early, not all mid-stage ventures are equally in the middle, and not all exits are mature. By the same token, not all multi-year commitments are equally appropriate.

5. Corporate finance in the age of options

Some businesses are good at revenues, and some are good at building options. (There is also a third category, that isn't good at either one, but this group doesn't beg as many questions.) Revenue in itself may not be the way to build enterprise value – to the extent that revenue models lead to a diminution of business optionality. The key, as always, is to know oneself. Which is to say, make a determination about the category in which your subject business belongs.

There is also another related determination. This has to do with independence versus dependence. Some businesses, some management teams, are meant to stand alone while others are not. An option does eventually have to be exercised, even if only in theory. In private enterprise and business building this means one of two things, and both of these lead to revenues. A platform based on pure potential has either to be sold to a platform that can afford to fund its promise and possibilities, or otherwise it must finance itself with actual cash. In the former scenario the acquirer will most likely be a business that is good at revenue and would benefit from a diversity of product, technology, and other open doors. In the latter case, and whether the cash is produced internally or acquired from outside, revenue does eventually have to jump into the fray.

So, to the list of determinations provided there is one more to add: timing. Timing of exit, timing of not exit, timing of revenue and timing of not, and, without getting too bogged down in the calculus of the value curve, timing of timing: Which is to say, knowing when to actively consider these matters and when to actively keep one's nose to the grindstone. It really isn't as complex as it sounds – most of this is just wordplay – and the listed determinations ought surely enough to resolve themselves naturally.

From the perspective of outside capital, however, where the assessment is one of financial valuation (often without a proper frame of reference in early venture stages) and structuring of terms to reflect an underlying enterprise risk, the old tried and true models are not necessarily the most useful. In the absence of revenue, discounted cash flow is not really any sort of tool beyond an academic what-if exercise. In the absence of optionality, a future value some years out can be precarious to say the least. (What was the future value of a cash flowing paging business around the mid-90s?) These are extreme examples to illustrate a point, whereas reality most regularly happens someplace in between – fortunately or unfortunately, depending on one's comfort with the task at hand.

In the last analysis, one should keep a steady but open mind today. Some of the financial theories we had learned don't wholly apply (ref. Benoit Mandelbrot), and some of the business building precepts we have taken for granted (e.g., revenues and related accounting) are not universal truths. Just as the study of economics should probably be updated these days by an industrial evolution that is increasingly information-centric, so also corporate finance should be filtered through the lens of an increasingly tech-driven ecosystem, the volatility of which may lead to value without revenues, as well as revenues without value.

6. The second way out

But if the business case doesn't work, how do we get out? Thus, the credit officer, the bane of my existence, back in the day. It was a time of leveraged buyouts, structures based on the decomposition of assets into isolated layers of risk. We dealt in the senior-most tranche of the cascade, the cheapest tranche because allegedly the most secure, the term loans and revolving lines that determined value for the swashbuckling private equity sponsors below. Books have been written about the era and the fabled financiers. Some of the deals made fortunes, (though not for senior debt providers). For some of us, though, the lessons have been priceless.

The theme resurfaced a decade later in a different context. It was the period when wireless networks were being built at a frenzied pace, when towers were popping up on highways, and attachments to roofs and the sides of buildings were blossoming in urban areas. Capital markets fed this engine, and the engine reciprocated with great fervor... until the banks pulled back. A deafening silence... through which – some of us recognizing the importance (and value opportunity) of keeping these network builds going – alternative funding sources were sought to fill the gap. The most logical target: real estate finance. The economics are basically the same, you see; there is a property, on land, and there are tenants with long-term leases signed.

Eh, no, I don't think so, we were told (back then). If the business case doesn't work, how do we get out? (My friend the credit officer would have been more than mildly amused.) In more traditional real estate, for instance, a hotel can be remodeled to be a hospital, a condominium complex can be made a resort, lots can be subdivided and sold off piecemeal, there are many possibilities and a few second ways. In a leveraged buyout, if cash flows miss the target then divisions can be divested or cut, inventory liquidated, something… But there aren't many alternatives in the mix for a tall piece of metal if its tenants fail to renew or some new technology emerges.

Now all these years later, the lessons of a finance past learned to the point of hardwiring, there are certain parallels one might consider in the funding of new ventures. On one hand it is almost a foregone conclusion that most digital technology startups will need at some point to "pivot," while on the other hand many of these startups are taken at face value in relation to their opening business case. A short while ago I noticed an article about the digital music sector with an illustration of its competitive landscape from five or six years ago, raising the question, where are they now? The digital music sector just happened to be the subject of this article, it could have been any other.

7. Signs of age as youth matures

Size matters. Stability, diversity and quality of product, capitalization, all matter. More and more so as technology, digital media, popular applications in commerce and elsewhere, evolve. If small and nimble are qualities at one extreme of a continuum that is bookended at the other side by heavy and dominant, the former traits are ideally suited for points of origin and times of high volatility. These are periods of constant change, multiple openings, and perpetually shifting opportunity. The latter set of qualities, conversely, will fare best in times of maturity, when making sharp turns is no longer part of the navigation.

This is a discussion about extremes, and the noted bookends are exactly that: absolute points of reference in a relative context. The extent to which connected systems and their adoption are closer to a point of origin or a point of maturity is debatable, but it's safe to say that the point of origin was not exactly yesterday. It's safe to say that the farther behind this point is left, the thinner the openings become and the harder the task of the upstart. By the same token, the clearer the point of maturity appears on the horizon, the greater the establishment's advantage. Again: A snapshot of extremes from a bigger picture that is relative.

And we can sometimes pick up clues about the state of affairs in industry by noting how capital behaves in its surroundings. Causes and effects are not always obvious, but the circumstance always bears watching.

Within the bigger universe of markets, capital directed at media, technology, information, and associated connected systems, comprises a sub-segment (which, according to the theory posited will in the long term take over and dominate). Until then, within this segment, here is a selection of observations from the latest patterns: (1) There has been venture capital consolidation, leading to fewer individual points with (often much) bigger pools to deploy; (2) there has been an increased emphasis on earnings and profitability for the post-IPO flagship properties, which have been severely penalized when the asset has not kept up with its optionality; (3) a great deal of M&A activity has been marked by small(ish) "acquihires" (that take out the upside of a startup before it has hit its stride) and integration purchases to round out the product portfolio of a large enterprise; (4) cash hoarding among the sector leaders has continued, and in many cases the cash is even diverted back to shareholders; and (5) there are pockets of growing interest in debt capital deployment, which is still limited but nevertheless notable for a sector traditionally marked by equity features and funding sources given to equity appetite.

While the sector and its markets are obviously in a state of evolution still, we can't lose sight of all that evolution brings as a byproduct with time. Size, stability, diversity and quality of product, and capitalization, all matter, and will more and more so as the points of origin and maturity become less equidistant.

8. When innovation is expected

The Innovator's Dilemma puts forth the idea that certain businesses fail precisely for acting properly. In these instances, a market-leading firm (or an established system, or a widely used technology) is disrupted by a new order not because the former had become too comfortable in the status quo but because the status quo was too comfortable in it. In other words, a quality product is being delivered in the best possible way to a satisfied market that expects the product it knows. The incumbent, thus, is doing its job.

All the while, innovation festers in the niches under the wide surface, and these percolating upstarts rise up to overturn market leadership by becoming widely accepted and dominant. The incumbent, who was beholden to a market, fails when the market changes its demands and allegiances. Then the cycle repeats for the new entrant; and the dilemma, thus, is about breaking the cycle while operating a successful established enterprise.

The described theory is built on several key assumptions. It presupposes a customer base that doesn't know it wants something until it is shown the way. ("If I had asked people what they wanted, they would have said faster horses," according to one fabled car innovator.) And it presupposes a contrast between novelty and repetition, between invention and the accepted state. On one hand, therefore, we are dealing with a market conditioned on establishment, and, on the other hand, a clear distinction, a gaping difference, between new and old orders.

Let's consider, though, to what extent these qualities still hold. In the past decade or more the rhythm of product introductions, new technologies, and related market growth, has been so fast that in many segments innovation is now the expectation. The establishment, in other words, is no longer surprised by invention but awaits it and takes it for granted. By the same token, novelty is less limited to niche targeting and adoption, or at least this isn't necessarily the case anymore, while some niches become mass market sensations in record time. One might even say that the marginal difference between new and old is on the whole no longer gaping.

Maybe it would be going too far to argue that the innovator's dilemma has been resolved – even as large corporations are dedicating capital and resources to the development of startups – but on a relative scale and at least in select industry segments, the issue is less pronounced. Or rather, the subject bears revisiting in a new context, which would be an exercise more than merely academic. Inherent in the theory are the definition of innovation, the requirements of markets, the expectation on modern enterprise and costs associated with satisfying these, the evolution of technology, and ultimately, the opportunities for investors.

One could make a case, I think, that we are entering a phase of economic development in which the invention of new technology is as much the domain of large enterprise as it is of new ventures. And one may also argue that strategic integration of new platforms into old, and incumbent systems with one another, are new forms of innovation in which the establishment (as much as the startup community and its backers) can be seen as new disrupters.

9. Where integrated systems lead

Now everyone is doing everything. And who can blame them? It's so cheap, on a relative scale, and it isn't even that hard, all things considered. It's not like launching a spacecraft, for instance. Besides, it's mobile, and mobile is where it's at, and where it's going. Google is making devices with location based customized search. Google is making NFC-based home entertainment units. Microsoft is rolling out tablets and Facebook has considered a phone. Apple has been there all along, and so Apple has to think about social and about search apps and the cloud. Everyone is thinking about that, and many are offering up their infrastructure as a service.

These observations are thrown together as such because of themes that emerge out of the mix. Some of these themes explain, and others are a consequence. Some just happen to be there and are worth a mention. For example, take the pattern of increasingly integrated hardware and software, particularly in mobile products. Apple introduced this tactic to some ridicule (which many now forget), and it has proven successful. While the competition has tried and is still trying to figure out how to monetize mobile – advertising isn't it for everyone – Apple has figure it out. It is hardware sales... Now everybody.

Another budding way to monetize mobile has been commerce. This isn't only mobile offers, although that too, but also other services, by subscription or otherwise. Foursquare is in that mix, as is Groupon, as is Square and other payment service providers, and one wonders if – or rather when – these will be acquired... and integrated... into someone's device. Apple has drawn up a sort of blueprint there as well, because mobile commerce integrated into mobile devices is more or less the definition of iTunes... No?

Only a matter of time before that becomes a ubiquitous payment solution. There are rumblings.

All of which leads us to a couple of other subjects of interest. If the pattern of integration, overlap and parallel direction should continue in linear fashion – but these things never do – then the result may be an increasingly segmented (rather than open) ecosystem. Each with its own device, its embedded network, its set of commerce applications, which won't necessarily communicate across platforms. (Is Twitter's disconnect with LinkedIn a sign? Is Apple's (attempted) removal of Google Maps in favor of its own product another example?) Should this occur – but these things are hardly ever cut-and-dry – consumers will have to pick favorites, and this will not be different, perhaps, from the selection of broadband or cable or telephone service provider.

The distinction between content and distribution – implied in the cited instances of distribution – would seem to favor premium content, particularly in an environment of integrated networks that resemble one another more and more. As content itself struggles to differentiate in an increasingly fragmented arena, maybe this too will be integrated at some point, maybe this too will turn exclusive to the network. That is a guess, only a guess, and not even that, more like a statement of possibility, but it follows the same general pattern of overlap and parallel paths and combinations. It also follows another theme, which has been the unspoken basis to all preceding observations:

An open environment is limited by its economics, and a self-imposed deflationary system (technology, in an otherwise inflationary economy) at some point will be forced to change course. Salaries and the rent have to be paid, investor returns must be generated, cash, at some point, does have to flow. Optionality, at some point, does expire, and there's an underlying asset that determines its exercise value. In a competitive field in which participants resemble one another more and more, so should their respective valuations. This last remark is one to which we may return at some point, after the dust begins to settle.

In any case, the medium is the new star. This idea will be revisited.

10. The idea and strategy: a new execution

If it is true that connected systems and their related media and technologies are moving towards a state of increased maturation – from an era defined by financial ventures to one that is highly strategic, from the more or less speculative to that which is structured, calculated, and framed within a narrower band of potential outcomes – then a significant offshoot will be the diminution of formula and the growth of creativity.

Stating the same thing in plainer language: In a period of rapid evolution and plentiful liquidity, when the terrain is relatively unharvested but fertile, there is incentive to build by imitation. If such-and-such works in Lot A, then find a different lot and implement the same. If there is gold in Lot B, then there are bound to be a few nuggets at least in its adjacencies. This is enterprise by formula and it is, if you will, algorithmic, mathematical.

When the frontier has been more fully explored and occupied, on the other hand, the opportunity for imitation declines. The many lots are now more likely harvested, the various methods more likely implemented, the marginal gold nugget now more difficult to find. Until a new frontier is discovered, the settlers have to get creative. This may involve joining forces, but not necessarily. It may involve finding new uses for older resources, or experimentation with different economic structures, or refocusing narrowly on select activities, or all these things, but not necessarily. This is no longer formula now, it is judgment call.

The adage that ideas come and go while execution is everything, this may still be true enough in the environment described, but the distinction between idea and execution is less sharp now. If we are no longer dealing with a land-grab, execution is less about the workhorse than its use, less about hyperventilation than planning, and trial-and-error iteration takes a different form. Strategy, in this context, is the new execution, and execution alone may not be worth what it once was. Data is no longer so big, but its interpretation, application, or discarding, will make all the difference.

To put it slightly differently still: Analog, so to speak, becomes the new digital, and the value of a technical degree stands to be enhanced by the MBA. Talking figuratively.

11. The path of data back to bigness

All invented products are at some point commoditized, and their value tends to diminution. The wheel was a premium asset at one time, no doubt. The cavemen and women showed it off as a point of pride, and they were envious of the neighbor's wheel: They talked disparagingly about it, and gave each other meaning glances. And look at the wheel now, we all have at least one, or did at one time or another, and we don't particularly care. It took a while to get to this point, and there were carriages and cars that came between the first wheel and the modern variation, but those carriages and cars too have lost their glimmer. The novelty at least is not what it once was. There aren't many invented products I can think of that don't follow this pattern – perhaps fire, which is to say, energy, but that's a different story. The subject of this chapter is big data.

The extent to which this field is truly new or is just now getting more widespread attention is debatable. Although the concept was perhaps around for many years, if not decades in one form or another, perhaps it now more truly "exists" because it has a name: Big Data. (It's catchy, a little bit like a fraternity brother's nickname, at least at some of the more technical schools.) Regardless of when the field was in actuality born, it's fair to say that it too, like other invented products before, is undergoing evolution. It is an enormously complex product – much more so than the wheel, at least in some ways – that incorporates issues of science as well as law, art as well as commerce, consumption as well as production. It is a highly specialized field, in which expertise is difficult to come by.

An initial conclusion that I draw – reserving the right to change my mind as the subject evolves and stabilizes – is that, like other invented products, big data is following an evolutionary path to its commoditization. From up in the clouds, the landscape and its horizon are looking roughly as follows:

Let's call the starting point *creation*, which is the collection or accumulation of massive amounts of data in a variety of on- and off-line platforms. The subsequent locale is *analysis*, an increasingly popular neighborhood of which is *visualization*. This allows our minds to extract meaning from otherwise impossible jumbles of raw information. Analysis has been with us since the point of creation, but visualization is now coming to its own, and it truly makes a world of difference: Images and symbols often convey a rich message, despite the seeming superficiality.

The next destination along the path is going to be *valuation*, which is not only an appraisal of product worth, but also a setting of *standards*. The two areas are closely related, and one drives the other as much as vice versa. While data is being collected and visualized, in many cases for the first time, we are still in a state of excitement, as it were, discovering new ways to play with this big data toy we now hold. Some of these ways will have not much more than entertainment value, while others will transcend the razzle-dazzle. As the distinction between the two and the nuances in between fall into place, so too will processes and procedures and standards of measure and accepted practice... And the next step from that – when the mystery and unlimited potential have been revealed and thus narrowed – is *price competition*: More generally termed, *commoditization*.

This is not to say that data will necessarily be bought or sold, although a lot of it will be and already is – directly or indirectly – but its relative merits, its differentiators, are prone to become standard. This follows the theme of all invented products, and it isn't to say that these turn obsolete. The wheel hasn't, but the differences between one wheel and another have turned minor. So too, a time may come when differences between one dataset and another will not be a matter of quality as much as quantity. If so, the label Big Data may prove to be more correct than we might currently imagine.

12. Too deep to fail

It's easiest to discuss gain and loss when dealing in tangible things, such as financial capital. Tangible things, however, are sometimes rooted in abstractions, and financial capital, for instance, is rooted in *information*. We should probably define our terms, and the definition of information is complicated, like any definition of abstractions. An entire Wikipedia page with its own table of contents is dedicated to the subject.

What I mean by information, for current purposes, is knowledge that is transferred or stored. And let's keep the discussion simple and stick to the idea of information as something very broad, containing everything from social gossip to ancient history, from global intelligence to the picture of a butterfly, from quantified data to Mona Lisa's smile (which, incidentally, I don't believe to contain as much knowledge as they claim). Let's say it's all information if it can be conveyed and processed.

With that established, the more important idea is the recognition of a growing and increasingly dominant footprint of information exchange. Facebook, Twitter, Google, Amazon and Yahoo! are participants in it, as are PayPal and ATM machines, as are Spotify and Netflix, as is the emerging *internet of things*. The samples and pieces may be distribution mechanisms or storage devices, computing processes and hardware; there are layers of security, targeting, and filter; there is the cloud; and there are countless other components in this deep and tangled web that increases (and at times reduces) knowledge, that influences our decisions and enjoyments, and compounds our risks.

The personal value of information is not a new idea, and its place in the individual and collective dynamic is all I've been writing about so far. But the notion of information loss, in this context, may not naturally occur to most of us. And the idea that losing valuable information can be equivalent to the loss of capital may not register to many beyond the fear of a broken hard-drive or identity theft.

What if, however, Facebook were to end? What if the Twitter servers were to lose your follows and followers? What if Spotify goes broke and with it your music library? In large part these examples and others relate to the perils of centralized storage, but the bigger issue here is that individually and as a collective we rely on the deposit of information much as we rely on the deposit of money in a bank. We take it for granted, we presuppose its safekeeping and its permanence.

As information exchanges mature in coming years, and as the world of information technology and media consolidates into its leadership core, concentrated pockets of information capital may emerge (and really already have), which will be responsible for the safekeeping of knowledge, if you will, almost as a public service. These will be information banks, knowledge repositories, the value of which will arguably be as important to protect as the old-fashioned other types of institutions that merely hold cash.

As we consider the fate of Google Reader, as we consider how and with whom we entrust our information, as we think about the interconnection of information and money flows, the themes presented should and probably will be in our consciousness more and more. As we consider the phenomenon of Bitcoin – a decentralized information-based currency – and Apple's staggering cash reserves, ideas about value storage and the safety of information deposits should probably also cross our minds.

13. Probability and flexibility

Pattern recognition, as some market watchers will attest, is more truly like pattern suspicion. In cases of analytic insistence there is even pattern creation, whereby the recognizer interprets information so as to fit a preconception. Suspicions and creations may in retrospect correspond with the actual pattern that was forming. At other times opportunities are wasted. But there is never a shortage of next chances to shine, because change is perpetual and thus new patterns are always around for the finding.

It is a question of probability really, as everyone knows, but also one of flexibility. The former relates to objective qualities, the latter to subjective interpretation. Inputs, outputs, meter readings, inspiration, and so on. There is science, and there's the art of overriding it. The override, of course, is how we sometimes get in trouble, but on the other hand it can also save us. Pattern recognition, in other words, is often about when and how to break with formula. When we do so, even successfully, we have created new formulas by definition, and it's a matter of time – maybe moments – before these might beg to be broken all over.

Probability and flexibility, as I said. On one hand to understand the limits of certainty, on the other to understand the limits of our tools: A prescription easier to acknowledge than adopt. Especially so in an era in which transformation and volatility seem perpetually to refresh patterns, while formulaic processes and mechanized reactions become an increasingly tempting solution to deal with the rapid-fire variables and inputs.

High frequency trading, programmatic advertising, algorithmic data processing, are advances as much as vulnerabilities in short-term action. Long-term strategy, necessitating long-term capital, is limited by externalities that may not follow the pattern initially conceived.

All directions require positioning for a frame of reference – whether short-term programmatic, long-term strategic, or any points around and in between – but positions would ideally contain the qualities described. Probability and flexibility come natural, unconsciously, in our every-day routines. The other things, the bigger ones, are not any less so. These are, however, more complex, and require consciousness and effort.

14. Adaptation as a specialty

Justice, according to one definition from antiquity, is carrying out one's duty to one's station. Plato did not strictly speaking have only professional specialization in mind, and he was probably not thinking about justice in the way we have come to think of justice. As a general rule, however, it was agreed that minding one's business and perfecting one's trade were positive attributes that would advance the health of a society. There is a lot to be said for this, even now, but it is also possible that Plato, who anticipated many things, did not anticipate convergence and falling barriers.

For several decades now of an economy that is increasingly powered by services, we have seen service providers increasingly compete on the basis of specialization. To play a generalist role, for example, in consulting, finance, law, medicine, may have its place, but is not nearly as valuable – when push comes to shove – as proving one's mettle in a concentrated domain. Because service providers tend to follow the course set by their clientele, for many specializations this pattern has been in imitation of underlying industries. A sector such as technology, for instance, that has included memory chips and turbine engines and biotech research and Google's algorithmic product, is clearly too vast to either operate or be served in a generalized fashion.

But the undercurrent now beginning to stir is causing some of these sectors to blend and overlap. Whether Amazon, say, is more properly speaking an Internet company or a consumer retailer, and whether the Internet is a sub-segment of technology or media, are increasingly fuzzy judgment calls. There used to be a distinction between traditional media and new media, but that's even going the way that apps and mobile access leads the two categories in tandem. Hardware and software are migrating towards one another as trends in open-source and 3-D printing take hold; and financial markets and information technology are converging to the point of unity. In the case of markets there even seems to be a movement of asset classes towards one another, as already discussed in previous chapters, as large institutions do smaller deals, as illiquid investments are made more liquid, and as the distinction between early- and late-stage diminishes and fizzles.

It's hard, in such an environment, to stay true to the Platonic ideal. And one might even say that to do so would be to do one's chosen field injustice. A narrow perspective, picked up in whatever classroom where one has continuously sat, becomes a constraining and counterproductive feature. But it is equally hard, on the other hand, to break the hyper-specialized mold in which so many of us have been shaped. This requires a perpetual education, re-education, and expansion. More than expertise, perhaps, success in such an environment is determined by one's ability to adapt.

And to take this argument one step further, this ability to adapt may be an expertise in itself, perhaps the most important there is, requiring hard work and special (re)training.

15. Panic and restraint*

* This is not an either/or idea. The title is not a show of extremes, but a formula for combination, a recipe for effectiveness in enterprise. Other than luck – which is not a recipe – this may be the only one I've seen consistently to work. There are probably others.

Panic may be too strong a word, but that's quibbling over semantics, (and urgency isn't nearly strong enough. You can brush your teeth with urgency.) But restraint is about right, though only combined with that first element in the mix. It's a tricky combination, quite delicate, a little like oil and water, and this is why some succeed and others don't. If it were easy, everyone would restrain panic, or hyperactivate restraint, or some such.

Implied in the message are two disparate themes. On one hand, it's very hard to make progress in enterprise if a healthy dose of fear is not perpetually present. Comfort is counterproductive, lack of sleep is recommended. Tossing and turning, queasiness, all good. We're in a fast-moving and highly unstable environment, for technology as well as its funding sources, and complacency doesn't even work in stodgy real estate. (What is recommended, indeed, is so far from complacency that even to invoke the word by contrast rings a false note.) As has been said, fear must be felt and nothing less. Your competitor who feels it most is the competitor you should fear the most. The opposite, by the way, is also true.

Unless and until, that is... such feelings can be taken to excess: Where terror leads to clouded judgment, poor decisions, pointless drivel, directionless stumbling about. There is a point where activity is not actually progress. Or worse, progress is made towards no goal, or some perpetually changing goal without reason, only fear. That is no good at all. That must be controlled and channeled. Like a water-hose, outflow and direction are both to be monitored, and this is an especially sensitive task when the underlying pressure is overwhelming.

Which reminds me of the slogan, "move fast and break things," popular in certain startups marked by growth. Time will tell, but I bet the formula gets revisited. Its intent to push a potentially comfortable organization to a greater urgency is commendable, to manufacture fear where there might otherwise have been false security. But history may show that the expansive growth brought on by a frenzied push was in parts illusive and some others reckless. Restraint may have been indicated. Flaws in a product mix, an enterprise direction, flaws in strategy, are hard to remedy because a business – unlike a stock – is an illiquid asset and big decisions can't simply be sold off.

Perhaps one day we will invent a system to break this illiquidity of business building, but I don't see that as a goal for which to strive. Able to hedge positions and exit our strategies easily, both our panic and our restraint would diminish. Without these things, the quality of enterprise would suffer and economic progress would, too. Without a healthy combination of panic and restraint, the results are prone to be familiar, and the outcome will be broken things indeed. We've seen it in the shape of a market, a street**, even a continent***.

** Wall   *** Europe

16. The secret of your success

The real find, the value, is between the digits and the lines of code. The truth is where formula can't find it. This isn't about high-frequency trading, nor financial gain, necessarily. Those are subclasses, indeed, but the bigger category is direction – where nuance and layers are the guideposts. Events, actions, possibilities, are rooted in rich reality even if our interpretation of it at times reduces its prospects. But eventually, maybe a long way ahead, misinterpretations are corrected.

If perception is in the present what defines our realities, then some realities are subject to change. Where an algorithm processes the immediate, based on formula, the opportunity lies in its eventual improvement.

Sometimes it is suggested that value emerges when the illiquid is liquefied. This doesn't only apply to venture capital exits or the reduction of illiquidity discounts in asset appraisals. Formulaic activity and algorithmic direction are also examples of rigidity that can be improved upon and made valuable with enhanced liquidity.

There is such a thing as liquidity of thought, (and also its inverse). In enterprise we have looked admiringly to the example of Steve Jobs and his many successes, all sharing that quality of something like shattered walls. In contrast, we see the image of certain competitors of Apple, which, at least for a while, had fallen into formulaic immobility.

The subject of idea liquidity is in essence the same as that of value created by breaking or fixing formulas. Steve Jobs's ability to see past preconceptions and artifice was similar, on one level, to that of an investor finding the untapped opportunity in an algorithmic environment. It requires the same largeness of perspective, the same spark of inspiration, the same artistic way of absorption and creation, of analysis and synthesis, in conflict or parallel. It's a mode that transcends formula, that only the human mind and spirit can channel, before the opportunity is tapped and we move on. The algorithm does not change itself, it needs redesign, and by the time this is noted it's probably a little late.

Success, on reflection, cannot be repeated. It is unique to the circumstance and one's happening upon the scene. There is no such thing as a serial entrepreneur. They are different people, and their successes or failures are surprising every time.

17. Before invention and execution

Invention is preceded by imitation, at least in the better examples. "Better" being a subjective qualifier, we can call these the more lasting inventions, the ones that have had the most profound impact. Such inventions have tended to be born after extended periods of learning and apprenticeship – and intense apprenticeship at that – for their inventors. There are exceptions, like the already mentioned case studies of fire and the wheel. But that's going pretty far back, and who is to say that the inventor of fire didn't spend years learning about the nature of sticks and friction. I was made to think about these notions by the entrepreneurs who populate the biographies I've been reading.

For example, John Adams and his colleagues, who invented a new form of government that to this day survives. According to David McCullough, the most prolific modern biographer of Adams, it was Adams who first presented an outline of what we now recognize as our system of executive, legislative (including two houses), and (independent) judicial branches, in an essay published long before the Declaration of Independence, let alone the Constitution. Before formulating such ideas – and at the time there was nothing to resemble the political structure proposed – John Adams had spent years and years in politics and law, and decades as a student. His knowledge of the classics and his bookishness are legendary, according to McCullough.

Among more pedestrian examples, there is a batch of subjects nearer and dearer to my own heart, the rock musicians turned authors. Before deigning to compose what we now know as the formative songs for generations of followers, these innovators of their time were first and foremost copycats. Keith Richards and The Rolling Stones were a rhythm & blues cover band for several years before they became the Glimmer Twins. Keith's first love, which was an ardent passion, was to learn how to *precisely* imitate the guitar sounds of Chuck Berry and Bo Diddley, among others. Each riff took hours of practice, and as a band the

Stones continued along the same pattern well into their fourth or fifth album.

It did not even occur to Bob Dylan to write original songs (can you imagine? never considered the possibility, this is Bob Dylan) until he had built a repertory of several hundred that he had learned from others. Unlike Keith Richards, this other apprentice did not seek to replicate note for note, but rather to discover fresh and newly expressive ways to interpret these hand-me-downs. In so doing, the performer was forced to pick apart every word, every nuance and inflection, and to dig through to the heart of every composition. Bob Dylan did not attend college, but his unofficially declared major was easily a doctorate, his term paper enormous.

With the backdrop of such instances of permanence and depth, we might reconsider our present-day breathlessness to start things up. We might revisit the rhythm and the scope of innovation in a time of maturation and convergence. If innovation is prone to mean something different now, compared to 40, 30, 20, 10, 5 years ago, then apprenticeship is necessary to find out what that is.

18. Rimbaud in Abyssinia: an entrepreneur's biography

By age 19 the subject has written all the poems he would ever write, which will revolutionize poetry for a century to come and influence art as varied as Henry Miller's memoirs and Patti Smith's CBGB's stage show. By age 27 he has traveled to all parts of the western hemisphere, in pursuit of business ventures. In his 30s, he settles in the remote city of Harar, in what is today Ethiopia, a landlocked ancient city where commerce had once thrived but is now slow, where prospects are few. More or less, this is where the story ends.

Reading this biographical travel guide, the author of which pursued an abbreviated route similar to that of Arthur Rimbaud in order to experience what his subject must have experienced, I was impressed by the similarities between Rimbaud in the 19th century and an entrepreneur of the present day. That entrepreneurship is a creative undertaking goes without saying, and one might even go so far as to compare the entrepreneur to the poet, as there is in many (perhaps most) entrepreneurs a spark of romance, idealism, inspiration, and the desire to touch – hopefully improve – some aspect of their environment.

What's more, there is an energy in entrepreneurship – a restlessness that is almost an end in itself – not dissimilar to the referenced poet's travel, his continuous quest, occasional discovery, and attempted invention. The story of Rimbaud's life is a catalog of calls to action. One might argue that his very poems even – innovative and meant to shake up the pervasive style – were a venture that had run its course... at which point the serial entrepreneur moved on... to his next projects in succession: commodities trading, gun running, (this was the 19th century, remember). These subsequent undertakings were no different in a sense from – and really a continuation of – "The Illuminations," "The Drunken Boat," "Season in Hell."

The tale, however, turns cautionary, as Rimbaud's storm and spark take him to a remote locale where he will meet his end. Considering, no doubt, Harar to be an "untapped market," the entrepreneur attacks it with his usual passion. But Harar, it seems, was fated to be untapped, and what seemed like a territory ripe for the entrepreneur's ventures turns out to be an isolated enclave where he is cut off from the flow of commerce, where conditions for business are poor (to say the least), and where, worst of all, there are few other business builders around.

And thus, it is once again demonstrated that no man is an island, and that context, timing, conditions, communication, interaction, traffic, learning, are all as important to an entrepreneur's success as are individual traits such as inspiration and energy. Rimbaud's classic poetry was a product of Paris, as much as it was of Rimbaud.

19. Skin in a portfolio of games

There's been a percolating debate at the economic fringes about the notion of "skin in the game." It is a complicated subject, like everything in economics, accompanied by its own analytics and mathematical models, which, like so much in economics, serve to prove beyond the shadow of doubt that common sense still dictates. To prove by algebra, as the saying goes, that such-and-such trails so-and-so in the causality of what-not, which isn't as circular a demonstration as one might assume on sight. The arguments, which have been fascinating, have led me to reflect on definitions. What, in the sense of the debate, constitutes "skin," and what actually is "the game"?

By way of background, the subject is centered on the notion that an opinion, a word of advice, a recommendation, a passionate conclusion in any field, but especially in one as complex as economics and markets, should be taken with a pinch of salt if the proponent is not also at risk of loss from following the recommended direction. The root of the debate (in which the advocates on both sides should ideally themselves be at risk of loss for being wrong) seems to be in the financial crisis and corresponding attention that banking and the banking system have garnered. But the same precepts could easily apply to other fields, directly or indirectly related. (Directly or indirectly, most fields lead to finance, banking and economics anyway.)

To keep to what I try to know best – which is to say, the topics that have recurred in this book over its pages – I look to the dynamic of capital markets and enterprise – fertile territory for "skin in the game" discussion. An entrepreneur, especially a founder, has got skin in his or her own game. An investor who manages his or her own money is at risk in the same way. From these extremes we look to their polar opposites, to employees and consultants, and then to variations and permutations between extremes. This grey area is where most of the world exists, and the greatest complexity is right there with it. To contemplate issues in terms of black and white may be useful as a guidepost, but we mustn't get stuck in that theoretical muck too long.

With this background, let's go back to the topic of definitions. *Skin*: The place where we feel pain and sometimes pleasure (though not the only place). In regard to this discussion, it is our ability to suffer or to benefit in proportion with the rightness or wrongness of our stated position. According to this definition, then, a few questions: Do gain and loss have the same meaning universally or is it relative to the individual case? And is the nature of the gain or loss to be measured in financial terms only, or could it contain other ingredients in whole or in combination, which may or may not be quantifiable?

Now, on to *game*: The theater in which the action happens, guided by certain rules of engagement. According to this definition, is the game identical for every player and every piece? Do all subjects and objects share the same experience and can their effectiveness be measured similarly?

To illustrate the complexity of these questions, and thus the murkiness of the idea, let's look to several scenarios from the every-day. Investors prefer to back operators who have already demonstrated their ability to succeed – yet, does each subsequent endeavor not become less crucial because there is less to lose in the broader context? And does not this same notion apply to fund managers as well, who are referred to as "investors" but who really take a fee for managing funds?

And now, this question is critical and universal: Where do we differentiate between an investor's skin and *talking one's book*? Is there not an incentive to promote a position, regardless of what it is, right or wrong, especially because one has skin in the game, and is one's genuineness not compromised for that very reason? Finally, how does one really differentiate these days between stakeholders in a game that is as fluid and as often arbitrary as the environment of convergence that has been described? We're really all invested in some shape or form.

And in the last analysis, given the intertwining and convolution (which only touch the iceberg's very tip), it is the portfolio that really matters; and we should probably think in terms of plural forms, say, skins in the game, or skin in the games, or some messy combination of both.

20. Dylan's playlist and pattern recognition

This last chapter is both business and pleasure, as has been the case all along, or for the most part, in this book. In the current installment, however, maybe more so... Youth is wasted on the young, and patterns can be hard to recognize up close. Bear with me, it might make sense in the end.

Bob Dylan played at my alma mater last weekend, at least two decades late. Back in the day, I would have sold my whole LP collection, not inconsiderable, to see him there. Eh, what can you do; as another alum liked to say, "so it goes." So it goes. But I was there in spirit! Very deeply so, floating in my faded jeans and loose black jacket, in homage to *The Last Waltz* style. So cool, almost aloof. Perhaps somebody saw me, I wouldn't be surprised.

Removed nevertheless, (though not necessarily detached), I have my own perspective of the show, based on a lifetime following the subject.

To begin, one needs to recognize and appreciate that the band currently playing has been together on a nearly perpetual tour since 1988. Because of the professional bond that develops, and to make such never-ending tour dates bearable for the musicians, the set-lists from one show to the next have tended to get shuffled and changed up on (Dylan's) whim. It keeps the music and musicians fresh... But during this present leg – almost entirely at college venues – the set-list is uniquely rigid, every show the same.

Is this important? In my opinion, yes, and in two ways:

Firstly, that the band was booked to play to college crowds on the kids' home-turf tells us that Dylan is reaching out to a new generation. Secondly, that the set-list is preselected and locked-in suggests that the content has been carefully thought through and chosen for a reason – not only the songs but also the order in which these are played. It amounts to the performance of a playlist, which is different from a set-list – a subtle distinction, but one that a generation raised on the iPod should understand.

So if the artist has put a bit of thought into this, let's humor the man and try to understand what he is saying to the kids. From where I sit, no longer one of them and admittedly removed, I see a pattern.

First off, I note the dearth of go-to "standards" in the mix; no Rolling Stone, no Memphis Blues, no Blowing in the Wind or Tambourine Man or any of that. Instead, a selection that most of the audience would not have heard in their family den or in the award-show inductions.

The lines within the song selection stir up nostalgia, resignation, irony, and related such motifs and fancies as an old man who has lived to tell the tale is likely to share with children who would listen. The show begins with "I used to care, but things have changed" ("don't get up, gentlemen, I'm only passing through"), runs its course through "This kind of love, I'm so sick of it," and "You can't open up your mind, boys, to every conceivable point of view" ("rough out there, high water everywhere"), a burlesque detour to those badass early Roman kings ("sluggers and muggers wearing fancy gold rings"), then back to the regretful Tangled Up In Blue ("we'll meet again someday on the avenue") and melancholic "beyond here lies nothing but the mountains of the past."

But the climax, the statement, arrives, as it should, towards the end, nearly there, before the encore's last notes. First, (from Thunder on the Mountain) "Been thinking about Alicia Keys, couldn't keep from crying, when she was born in Hell's Kitchen I was living down the line, I'm wondering where in the world Alicia Keys could be," sets up the punch line. And by thematic extension, the next tune, Scarlet Town, takes it home:

"All things are beautiful in their time..."

All things are beautiful in their time... Remembering that Dylan is singing to the young, the new generation, one really has to pause right here in order to sigh.

The ballad of Mr. Jones (I assume, the encore) closes the show on a familiar note, sending the students back to libraries and study halls to "read all of F. Scott Fitzgerald's books," as they should.

The thing about pattern recognition is that it can be rather subjective, and we often project ourselves into patterns we think we recognize. By the same token, there are patterns that can only really be seen through subjectivity. Machine learning, predictive analytics, natural language processing, and all such algorithmic fare have their limits. Digital technology is binary, and by definition bound by two whole numbers. These sharp numeric tools do not pick up on the patterns we occasionally notice, because formula is void of character. It's the analog interpretations, even when flawed, that shape our choices and definitions.

I wonder, as Bob Dylan looked into the crowd of lit-up iPhones what patterns he thought he recognized. A quantitative set of filters will not quite calculate the answer, and the targeted message sent wirelessly our way will be misplaced.

In my next installments of material, I'll return to normal and customary fare. I'm thinking, something about the meaning of disruption and knowing when to exit.

Appendices & Notes

Products & Other Enticements

1. Customers and code in networks

The concept of networks is not new, but the way we think about networks is. We tend now to think of networks as social networks, and when we do so we think of connections and followers and friends in a densely interconnected web. The emergence of LinkedIn and Twitter and Facebook and other such platforms that interconnect most of the connected world is causing our perception to change, but the meaning of the concept is as old and fundamental as the marketplace. At its core, a network is a community. Generally, the community's participants depend on one another for the community's survival, and sometimes they only depend on a single core, a nucleus, which itself depends on the participants' support.

When the final episode of Seinfeld aired, there was a cluster around the television monitor at the LAX gate where we all watched together. The assemblage around the water-cooler on Friday mornings, after each previous night's episode, had been a massive "graph" for a decade. The enormity of this community enabled advertising commerce easily as effective as any Google Circle. (The distribution vehicle for the show was network television, a word choice we took for granted then.) PayPal, to use another example, is a network, too, with a web of participants as intertwined as a phone system. And for that matter, if we stop to reflect, we see networks all around us: A sports franchise and its fan base, a university and its alumni, a health maintenance organization, and would it be too much to include the assemblage of Starbucks outlets?

In all these cases there is a glue, a common thread that keeps the multitude together. The network operator's task is always to strengthen the thread and to enhance the glue's stickiness. Sports franchises try to win, network television reshuffles lineups, HMOs mandate cross-referrals, Starbucks introduces new flavors and ways to pass the time, editors work on their blog comment sections, payment networks expand their ubiquity with mobile apps and point of sale systems, branch banking (let's not forget this network) hands out toasters and online account integration.

Even if we limit ourselves to the strictly modern and mobile web-enabled understanding of the network concept, we see community building well beyond Facebook, LinkedIn, Twitter, and the conventionally social others. Google keeps adding features to its Gmail product for a reason. So too has Apple integrated multiple devices with a unique entertainment experience and a physical retail presence. Speaking of retail, Amazon gives its customers less and less reason to shop anywhere else while adding to its network of independent merchants. Microsoft (whose Windows product was perhaps the original digital network) has set out in almost all these directions. And Tesla is building a national network of refill stations for its community of automotive customers.

The concept, again, isn't new. The first shopkeeper thought of these angles. (Actually, not the first, but the second, and then the first reacted.) The idea of communities is as old as the idea of repeat-business; the power of networks as old as the invention of cities. As long as there is value in community, magnitude is but one piece and technology a component. Quality of traffic and its recurring return are the thing; bridges and moats build and preserve these bases. Customer knowledge, more than code, engineers these necessary structures. The founder of the world's most bridged and moated network provides us with an excellent example.

2. The switches are different now

Necessity, inertia and fickleness are points along the same continuum of consumption. We talk about network effect when we talk about some of these points, and there is the notion of switching cost when we talk about some others. These may be separate points, but these are also related. If network effect is a positive attribute – a quality based on value offered – then switching cost is defensive and almost negative: One is reason to stay, the other one not to leave. When options are plentiful and often interchangeable, the distinction between these is vague and maybe inconsequential. By the same token, a vendor in a plentiful and increasingly undifferentiated market has to consider these yings and yangs with increased care.

In the four spheres of media – social, information, entertainment and transactional – we look to Facebook, Google, Apple and Amazon respectively for illustration. That Facebook benefits from network effect is an essential given, and after years of building one's user profile and accumulating associations, a subscriber's cost to discontinue is almost frighteningly palpable. The other three have networks of their own, and strategies to combat switching that go hand in glove. Though perhaps less obvious, these often have to do with hardware and software combination, or with the blending of other seemingly disparate codependences: payment systems, messaging tools, email protocols, recommendation engines, file storage, devices and retail outlets, and other imaginative ways of building dependence in an otherwise commoditized environment.

An iTunes library, for example, is something you wouldn't want to lose, and when access to this is consolidated across multiple devices – iPhone, iPad, iPod, MacBook – you probably don't want to lose those either. You probably want to upgrade, in fact, and visit the Apple store on occasion to keep up with the latest. This is network effect as well, in a sense, and now that iMessages are being rolled out across the spectrum of products, the network is no longer merely proverbial. Seen in this manner, Amazon's aggressive move into hardware and integrated software and eBooks and now also a store outlet is almost a perfect replica. With this backdrop, again, Gmail and Wallet and Drive and all the other apps and paraphernalia in the Android ecosystem are a collection of hooks to grab us back. A time may come when a more popular search experience is introduced elsewhere, and then these hooks could really prove their mettle.

As one considers these and related sector trends – strategies pursued and behavior noted – the thought solidifies that social is not the only network in our popular domain. The observation also registers that our older networks – the telephone and cable systems – are steadily losing pieces of cachet. This may leads us to conclude thusly:

In an environment of product invention on one hand and commoditization on the other, network effect requires constant nurture, and switching costs have always to be grown.

3. The origins and ends of communities

The idea of specialization in networks has been manifesting itself with growing regularity and in multiple locations. Just the other day a columnist questioned whether a service like Quora can be truly for the masses, or whether it is fated to remain of special status as a club of garrulous techies and other web aficionados essentially conversing with each other. Perhaps this is going too far, but the idea is anyway not about insularity as much as it is about niche. It is about a unique value proposition in a vast web community with multiple facets.

A variation on this theme was noted on a popular blog a longer time ago, in a post about the existence of multiple social graphs for different aspects of life. Among other subjects of that article was the inclination of those within the social web to use different networks, different services, for different reasons. LinkedIn, for example, professionally; Twitter to collect information; Facebook to connect with friends online; Foursquare to connect with friends in person. There, once again, the principle was implicitly challenged, that one network (even Facebook) can adequately cover all of our social bases; and the notion of necessary niches was thus again put forth.

In both of these instances – arguing the case for network specialization – one comes away wondering why the reality of networks, (agreeing as I do with the respective authors), is that way. Why do we gravitate to one social interaction for one purpose and to another for another? Functionality plays a big role, no doubt: For example, Twitter (until recently) used to be a clunky picture sharing service while Facebook was much more effective. But this is not always an accurate segmentation, and oftentimes characteristics overlap: tweets and updates are not very different, and if one really wished it one could create a personal LinkedIn profile that would downplay the prescribed professional formula. By the same token, discussion topics are found on LinkedIn in ways not dissimilar to questions on Quora; and people can be followed on Quora just as they can be on other networks.

I realize that there are differences of nuance in each of the examples cited, but I question to what extent such differences are the cause or the effect of our custom. Why don't we use LinkedIn updates interchangeably with tweets? Well, in fact, many of us do, and truth be told, it's a little bit annoying. I have no problem scrolling past endless drivel on Twitter, but I wouldn't do so with the same forgiveness on LinkedIn. It is a personal quirk, maybe, but maybe it also speaks to how we become conditioned, and how our expectations are established.

With such reflections I begin to think that there is more arbitrariness to the way social networks emerge than we realize, and that the rigid functionality of our social networking experience is formed at the very origin of these. We use Facebook the way we do because we always have; we use Twitter the way we always will; we ask certain questions on Quora rather than LinkedIn because it is expected. These are all habits that have been formed, and that will not be altered. Any new use, any new social graph, will thus require a new network. Many subscribers still pay Aol a fee to use their dial-up service, because that's what these subscribers have always done. Yet few still think to visit MySpace, which is free of charge.

4. Evaluating a big network, which isn't a big product

The event that defined our network era was, according to the world, upon us. Maybe its significance was not actually as monumental as all that – considering others that have at least shaped finance in our time – but beyond the panache of an opening line there is an element of truth to the statement. There are approximately seven billion people on this planet, and more than one of every seven (including newborns and residents of remote unconnected places) are registered on Facebook. When Facebook prepared for its initial public offering, this was almost a redundancy. And while its IPO may not be as consequential as, say, TARP or QE rounds or LTRO, or all the littler happenings that led up to those trillion-dollar items, Facebook is as real a symbol of our era as any bailout; on some level, perhaps, these symbols are anyway all intertwined.

The reason for the introductory bombast is more than stylistic, and really quite substantive; it has to do with valuation. As the punditry were circulating financial metrics and operating assumptions, seeking to benchmark these against an expected $75-100 billion reported value range, I figured that this missed the point. Because Facebook is not merely a large business, or merely a dominant product, but rather a global network with its precedent elsewhere. Were Facebook a growing and substantial business alone, were it a utility only, then revenue multiples and such conventional analysis would apply. As a global interconnection of massive scale, however, as a standard of interpersonal communication – like, possibly, the telephone or email before it – conventional analysis is rendered secondary.

Let's assume for a moment that Facebook's current revenue model collapses immediately. Let's assume that advertising goes away. Does this mean that a network of more than one billion registered users has lost its value? This would imply that the value of a global network of such scale resides within the confines of foreseeable business prospects, which begs the following question:

If email or phone technology were owned by one entity, would its current monetization mechanism really matter or would its existence alone suffice? The rhetorical point being this: A network transcends fleeting business models and products that come and go. A network makes business and products possible, and it can't be circumvented.

Valuing such a thing, putting a number to it precisely, is no easy feat. If absolutely pressed, I'd be inclined to go with something like a customer lifetime value calculation, but staring into the unknown. I would ask myself: How much, on a present value basis, would the total of all current and future entities in this world pay Facebook to gain access to its average current user? This is overly simplistic, of course, because the user base grows and also churns with time, and a lot depends on which of these outpaces the other. A lot also depends on the cost to maintain the user base and secure the network, whether growing or shrinking, and capital cost plays a circular sort of role in the calculation, as always. It is not an easy trip, like I said, but we should at least start on the proper track, in the correct direction; and conventional metrics aren't always and forever appropriate.

5. Value and renewal of used assets

The more some things change, the more these become familiar. Technical advancement has throughout history changed rules of engagement, but the rules of commerce tend to be what they have always been. The logic of markups, markdowns, inventory management is generally consistent for online and offline retail, even if systems are different. The goal of increased traffic is the same for merchants in this century as it was for merchants in the last, even if methods vary. Advertising, marketing, promotions, whether on paper, in the mail, on television, radio, billboards, or on mobile devices, deliver similar messages and are driven by the same fundamental business needs, regardless of industry or era.

And regardless of technology or automation, the most valuable business asset tends one way or another to boil down to customer relationships. In media, which uniquely brings together merchants and customers, this is about community and following.

When innovative platforms such as, for instance, Groupon, blend new technology and direct sales to build networks of local sellers and buyers, this is not fundamentally different from what local media platforms have done for decades... or, in the case of newspapers, centuries. When social networks like LinkedIn combine individual information and professional interests with company profiles and contacts, this is only a stone's throw away from the classifieds. Newsfeeds intermingled with the occasional sponsored ad on Twitter is news media in its most fundamental form, only mobile and more immediate than Twitter's more traditional counterparts. Facebook, which is attempting to do more or less all of the above, is in this sense a sort of media conglomerate, even if it is still tinkering and experimenting with various recipes of advertising, promotions and direct commerce. What all these new platforms rely on and strive for – communities of engaged users – is something the traditional media have built and nurtured since forever.

Despite such parallels and similarities, there seems to be a lapse in perception and certainly in financial valuation, between the new and the more traditional media. Up to this point, the contrast has been justified. On one hand there are new technologies demonstrating enormous user adoption and global growth, while on the other hand there are mature businesses. On one hand there is a high option value, as innovation finds its place on volatile terrain, while on the other hand there is the tried and true and that which – according to perception – "is what it is," or, more appropriately perhaps, what it was. We now seem, however, to find ourselves at a point where certain changes in environment are discernible, and which have the potential to change the dynamic described. On one hand, sector volatility is subsiding – which is to say, the newer media leaders are establishing their presence and drawing up their domains, while consumers are beginning to settle into seemingly lasting habits. On the other hand, new technologies – especially in data and targeting – are enabling new efficiencies to be extracted from large existing user bases in media consumption.

In short, the option value now is not necessarily – or not only – in the new platform with its new users, but also in new ways to access existing networks and tap into existing product. The newest opportunity, in other words, and one that is likely to last for some time, is for traditional media to incorporate new systems into its massive engaged networks already in place, and for the new media establishment to integrate older platforms and tap into enormous existing potential. Stated differently still, the new optionality and value creation opportunity in media – whether new or old – lies in the integration of established user networks with new technologies. In this new landscape, there is as much untapped value in traditional media, the audiences of which are as massive and as engaged as any of their newer counterparts.

6. Information in the physical world

To a large extent in these discussions there is the understanding that information – synonymous with knowledge and, in the more technical sense, data – is to be approached almost in the abstract, as a concept, or, most materially speaking, a set of bits. This isn't to say that the reality of information isn't as thick as that of ice cubes, but we tend not to associate information with the physical world quite as directly as stirring up a drink.

The physical world, however, is not only where all information is produced, processed, and put to work, but where knowledge morphs into its material manifestations.

Increasingly these days the morphing is not so much an evolution or progression as it is an actual overlap. The worlds of the abstract and the physical are combining not only in the analytic sense but in the very substance of physical reality and performance.

The self-driving car is as clear a representation as any of the merger between information and metal, as are robotic assembly lines in some related manufacture. The printing of physical objects, the monitoring of physical health, the processing of physical commerce, these are more than instances of hardware and software integration. These are examples of information and three-dimensional substance combining.

In some ways this was always the case. Wittingly or not, a toothbrush combines information with utility in a physical object. But there is always a broker in the transaction, a human intermediary. When the toothbrush is able to optimize the number of strokes and correct their angle on its own, this combination is a new object altogether and the disintermediation that occurs is a new event to be noted.

The consequences and repercussions of the toothbrush example – which was made up to illustrate on a small scale a bigger and much more than trivial point – will not be limited to personal hygiene. As information processing and technology enter the physical world in a very real way, the place of the individual in relation to the real world is altered. (The world itself, made up of individuals, changes.) In this example it was referred to as a disintermediation – maybe that's one way of looking at it. For sure there are others, and these are going to cross into multiple fields.

The self-driving car – a real example that many predict to become a commonplace mass-market product within a decade or so – has the potential to change not only personal habits but also city planning, for starters. It has the potential to make both the DMV and cabbies obsolete. It will impact the way we think about travel and commuting, and what we do during our commute. In just this handful of speculations there is sociology, psychology, culture, politics, and that which always tends to tie these together in a jumbled and lopsided package: economics. Less intensely, the changes have already begun.

7. The human factor

Data, we have data. We have programs to sort it. We have imaging to show it. We have machines to act on it. In financial markets data is dissected in millisecond increments. In commerce data is collected in unspeakable megabyte exponents. Data is hunted, courted, jealously guarded, sold, traded. It's all the rage. It is almost as though data were knowledge. (They say knowledge is power, I think that's what they say, although I could be wrong, they say many things.) But data is not knowledge. Data is numbers, strings, symbols of some variety. At best it is visualized, or, say, interpreted. Even then, it is at best a message. (And it could be wrong.) What now? What after data?

From all this true or false, valuable or worthless, information, disinformation, statistics, and not-knowledge, there must be processing, understanding, action. You see a sign, it says 44, or Phoenix, or turn right. What does this mean outside of context? What do you do even when the context is understood? Do you turn right, are you sure? Because you're trying to get to Phoenix? What's there? Why not Vegas? Maybe the number 44 has more substance at the tables than on the road, even if the distance is greater. But all of this is esoterica, it is to illustrate a general case. We can get into specifics, which, like data, wouldn't be comprehensive.

For instance, in financial markets there are tools to scour public text, picking up information before others can. And then some trader wins the day – just as an example, or maybe a finance undergraduate – because they notice an interesting choice of words in the filing of a certain bank. Note, it's the nuance, the combination of word selection with some other piece of information, not either of these in isolation.

Or in commerce, say, data indicates that a certain product at a particular discount in a particular place on the shelf sells more units on weekend mornings than weekday afternoons. What now? And what about season and weather, what about other products on the shelf, and most importantly, the store manager? (Many of these variables carry over to online commerce, even if the store manager is, arguably, more virtual there.) Then there are issues of design. Apple products, for instance, fly off the shelves no matter what Best Buy does.

A favorite example, to which I always come back, combining the use of data with business in a highly visible way, is popular sports. Take NBA basketball. All player data in the world – rebounds, assists, blocked shots, points in the paint per 48 minutes, 3-point field-goal percentage in the fourth quarter – even if adjusted for salary cap limits and loopholes and draft positioning, cannot predict a championship. This being about fitting pieces, and team chemistry, and effort, in the last analysis.

The point of these examples, which are isolated and not to be taken out of context, is in part to draw attention to the importance of context itself. It is to highlight the functionality of argument and interpretation. It is to draw attention to slippery nuance. Finally, it is to shine a light on the infinity of variables that impact outcomes, the dimensions of which can never be fully calculated by data, even in its most visual and interpreted form. In short, this is about the unique (and perhaps rising) value of analog product in an increasingly digital environment. This is about the place of arts in an industry dominated by science, and of insight in a market crowded with formula.

Ultimately, these arguments take us to a place where data, in all its bigness, is not an end, not even a middle really, but only one beginning. One. From here the impact of the action isn't derivative, as in calculus, but more properly sequential, as in history. The most valuable information, again, is not the data – which will be a commodity before long, and maybe is already – but the advice. The most valuable asset, in the last analysis, is not the technology, but the network. The most significant voice, in this environment, is not that of the individual, but that of the collective, the platform, and the medium.

8. So you wanna be...

This is the era where everybody creates... Here are two venture-backed companies, united only by investor portfolio. One is a 3D-printing platform and the other a digital sound network: one is physical and the other is virtual. These have paired in the introduction of a new consumer offer: Submit a digital sound sequence – the segment of a song, for instance – and see this converted to a practical object, say an iPhone case.

Consider the levels of creativity taking place: The creation of sound by an artist, the selection of sound by a consumer, the design of an individual object, its unique production by a machine, and finally, the creative combination of two companies that are only related by investor portfolio. The chain is tied neatly together in commerce, and perhaps one other portfolio company could creatively serve as an outlet.

The instinct for self-expression that is the creative instinct is the defining aspect of social networks. Whether we share our interests and activities on one, our professional profile on another, our news stream on still a third, or our pictures and our songs and our objects of desire, these are all aspects of ourselves and the social networking activity is our calling out.

It used to be an exclusive circle, where entry was permitted only to the starving artists, but this has been democratized and now the starvation is widespread. This is to say, whereas media was once a dissemination of messages from few to many, it is now a network (many to many) and the value of individual content is as a result diminished: Supply and demand, fragmentation, commoditization, and so on. This is the era where everybody creates...

There are two parallel tracks contained in the broader movement. On one hand, *the medium is the new star*; and on the other hand advertising is displaced by direct commerce. The two hands are closely related, and it couldn't happen any other way. See how one begets the other: If media was conceived as a platform for merchants to sell their wares, in which creative content was only incidental – to attract attention – and advertising was the true message and scope, then the fragmented cheapening of content leads to a fragmented cheapening of advertising, while the social networks become core to (a more effective) direct exchange. Groupon, you know, didn't happen out of nowhere. Foursquare, like any network, is also self-expression. In networks, buyers and sellers converge, and, arguably, content and advertising are one. This is the era where everybody creates...

When Patti Smith improvised those lyrics in the middle of covering the classic Byrds tune, she was promoting records and she was anticipating social commerce as a form of self-expression and sales. She was also describing a quality – *so you wanna be a rock'n'roll star*, perhaps more characteristic to our era than others – of individual ambition for stardom. This makes us the perfect promotional device, and it makes social media both a cause and effect in an era where everybody creates.

"Recognize my face? They call me broken glass... That's because... of the sound... of my voice." I love that, I'm going to get an iPhone case to look just like that fragment, and I will send messages and pictures from my gadget and tell everyone all about myself.

9. Of pictures and the true value of pixel sharing

Absorption and expression are associated by more than sequence and causality, these are in some ways synonymous. The act of reading and the act of writing are interlinked, just as looking and showing are part of the same inclination. Taking a picture forces us to concentrate on its subject, and it's debatable whether photography is analogous to reading or to writing, or to both in different ways. The value (for many) in jotting down ideas – for instance, in a blog post – is in the act of learning. It's in the process of gathering one's thoughts and sharing these in a concise and logical flow that hopefully resembles truth; just as the process of taking a picture, in the same way, is like an act of seeing. This isn't as easy as it sounds, it shouldn't be taken for granted. We look around us all the time, and we occasionally see.

The value of social media, in this way of thinking, is partly educational. The merest tweet forces its author to think. The most trivial Instagram snapshot forces its photographer to see. Even the falsest Facebook profile is the result of creativity. The self-expression at the core of such activities – within reason, naturally, and not all in the same way or to the same degree – is a mental exercise of measurable value. A trivial tweet may be a missed opportunity, as would be a careless photograph, but neither of these actions is as wasteful as reading or seeing the result superficially. In other words, beauty is in the eye of its creator, and that is a whole other can of worms…

Like many scribbles around the time of this initial writing, it led to the iPad's retina display. I hadn't seen it yet, but I felt as though I had. So much had been said about the wonder of its pixels, I looked for pixels everywhere. I'm typing now and as the letters appear on my screen I feel a little bit jilted that the shapes don't burst with flash. I look down at the keyboard and I think, how much better the plastic would appear if made of many tiny light-bulbs to accentuate it. Don't get me started about my chair, that piece of wooden garbage could really use a pixel makeover. I sure would like to see it in high-def, with cracks and all, it would make the sitting experience a new thrill always, might even make the wood somehow softer. If I had a new iPad with its retina display, I don't think I would ever look away.

This is an exaggeration, as was the prior sequence about the educational merits of a trivial tweet, but in exaggeration some random truth here and there is prone to surface. I don't know what that truth is quite yet, but I'm nagged by the thought that the iPad's visual extravaganza and social media are at polar ends of the same continuum – where the former is almost escapist, while the latter is concentrated reality – and that's probably an exaggeration also.

This is all strictly relative, and it's certainly not a contest of one versus the other. The two obviously coexist, and maybe enhance one another in ways. But this duality of escapism and reality, of bright pixels for all and creativity for the individual, could merit additional reflection. I stumbled upon the notion while messing around on my keyboard and staring at a screen that seems almost analog to me now.

10. The world as will and representation

The title refers to a very long story, don't ask. It's doubtful that when Schopenhauer penciled in his treatise he was anticipating Pinterest, although I can't vouch for anyone's anticipations, least of all Schopenhauer's. Regardless of all that, the author was so prescient that the only way to have described social media more precisely would have been to draft up a chapter on Facebook. In fairness, *will* has been a fixture in the world since forever, but *representation* has sure come up fast. And there could not have been so strong a hint of its potential in 19th century Germany. Let's give credit where it is due: Schopenhauer understood his market. Like Zuckerberg, he had his finger on the pulse.

This post, however, is not about Schopenhauer, not per se, but rather about data and commerce, some aspects of security, and the association these all have to advertising (with media as go-between). At one time there was something of a ritual, a game of sorts, in which the merchant-pursuer courted the consumer-pursued while the latter hid modestly behind a curtain, listening to pebbles tossed against the glass from below. Blip, yoo-hoo, reveal yourself, see the merchandise I bring to you. Occasionally the curtain might stir, signaling impatience, or maybe that the message was heard, and maybe – but this was more than the pebble-tosser could hope – that the merchandise being studied. There was a mystery to the affair, and the will of the consumer was revealed only in measures. That was before representation really took off.

The consumer-pursued, in a reversal of roles, is now turning to unabashed pursuer. The curtain is pulled wide and the presence that was previously mysterious and delicate is chucking blunt objects back at the merchant. No hints and giggles, no side glances, but a loud show of interest, whack, I want this and that and I want my friends to want these also. The world as will and representation, like I said, and Schopenhauer couldn't have scripted the scene more clearly.

Again, this leads us to consider data and measurement, the safeguarding of consumer information, and the association these have to commerce (with media as go-between). In the days of modesty, when the consumer-pursued played games with merchant-pursuers, the role of data would have been to draw down clues of what went on behind those stirring curtains, and security (among other things) closed windows and wrapped curtains tight up there behind the glass. (The past tense, incidentally, is used for effect – these things are kind of still present – but Pinterest may be providing us with glimpses of what could lie ahead.) If we extrapolate out to a futuristic era in which the windows are swung open and the rocks fly down with fervent precision to let merchants know precisely what's expected and when, then the roles of pursuer and pursued may not be the only reversals we will witness. The supporting cast – data, and that which would keep merchants from getting it – may also be reconfigured.

When the consumer doesn't want to hide, when buyer chases vendor without hesitation, then maybe data turns into a tool for shoppers. When representation is less a process for advertising but a demonstration of consumer will, the veils too may change from one side to the other. While rules of engagement may very well be absolute, the direction of these – such as, for instance, the path that leads from will out to its sequence of representations – is often relative, and might even change course every so often.

11. The medium is the new star

To make a long story short, it seems as though the value of content, (and in some ways even its role), and that of distribution, have reversed. This is not reflective of any market research, and I won't be held to the anecdotal value of my observations, but I speak here from serious experience and attentive scoping.

Whereas we used to hang around the water cooler Friday mornings to talk about the Seinfeld episode of the night before, the truly hip and with it are now more likely to talk about their home networking setup that allows them to watch Seinfeld in multiple languages at all hours any day, with the musical soundtrack of their choosing. Whereas we used to wear all sorts of shirts and promotional garb featuring the emblem or the picture of our favorite rock'n'roll idol, we are now more likely to show off our Android or iPhone or MacBook Pro, on which, true enough, there is a playlist featuring some idol betwixt all manner of other virtual possessions. Whereas we used to leaf through the pages of certain authors riding on subways or sitting in cafes, an act in which the book-cover served a function similar to that of a concert t-shirt, we are now more likely to hide that cover inside the neutralizing and anonymous Kindle. And we don the Kindle with pride.

As already stated, these observations aren't scientific, but I would bet that somewhere there is a focus group that, even as I write this, is voting in favor of a free iPhone over the complete Beatles collection. Feel free to substitute some other subject in place of the Beatles, it doesn't matter, the result would be no different for the focus group that is my instinct.

I am reminded about the widely circulated email response from Steve Jobs, at one time, to a long but humble and doting letter, composed by one of his fans – a gentleman who had built his entire business around Apple products. In this letter, Jobs is asked to please intervene on the fellow's behalf and see that Apple's lawyers dismiss their complaint against his company for naming its most popular product something that resembles the iPod. After all, this works in conjunction with iPods, he explains, and has for more than 5 years made the iPod a more versatile product (at no cost to Apple). On and on the letter goes, with paragraphs of justification, recitation and pleading.

After a pause, the stage-lights dim, the voice steps up to the mike: "Just change your apps name. Not that big of a deal."

Signed, "Steve
Sent from my iPhone"…

Lights flash, the guitars blast, the crowd goes wild.

New Economies & Markets

1. The hack, the shakeup, and the flourish

We tear things down and then we build them up again. After hackers who started out deconstructing the telephone and its network grid – in order to build calculating machines that eventually became personal computers – much of the hacking taking place today is informational. Systems are decomposed and rebuilt, elements fragmented and combined. The hacker's glory is in the possibility itself, the option, more than the novelty from which it stems or where it leads.

This new teardown is leading to buildups of redefined and combined media segments. Convergences without – between media and commerce, between media and finance, between finance and commerce – are wrapped up tightly with a tape that is the information and its flows. Convergences within – between the spheres of social, entertainment, transactional, and informational media itself – are glued and firmed up by the data. Which all in the end returns to commerce, that field where information is harvested and made into nourishment.

In contrast with such combinational motifs and cross-segment tendencies there is an opposing movement underway. This has to do with dispersal and fragmentation, with outward trajectory and ubiquity (rather than consolidation and concentrated centers). This is about breaking walls and spreading out multitudes. Made possible by faster, easier, cheaper information access, based on its efficient collection, analysis and presentation, previously capital-intensive and necessarily concentrated structures are moving towards a democratization built on foundations of knowledge.

The theme is quite pronounced in finance and markets – in credit and analysis, in research and investment, in payments and processing, in the matching of buyers and sellers – where in the end, the transaction follows the data and its corollary in security. These categories and subcategories, thus, are also brought to and rotate around a central core of information, which also rises and descends, spins and turns, but in the end comes back to commerce: from where it was first harvested.

If we come to see media pragmatically, as a platform for commerce, where advertising and transactions aren't byproducts but the very purpose, then we also see how finance and its markets – essential as these are to commercial flow – follow a natural path in the movements described. And so, as hackers continue to hack and information continues to travel, the next migration (beginning to get noticed already) will not be as technical as maybe geographical, at least symbolically: Behold the monuments that are Wall Street, Madison Avenue, Silicon Valley, and Hollywood.

Behold the evolution of all four and their convergence. Behold the most monumental of all hacks that, in the not too distant future, is likely to emerge and blossom:

The future bank will be a media conglomerate. The seeds of possibility have been sown.

2. How seemingly disparate markets are born of the same misconception

Option value and financial leverage are in a way two sides of the same coin. If the value of a business can be decomposed into its asset and its optionality, then debt obligations should be linked to the asset, and equity to the option. This is an oversimplification which may do injustice to business value, assets, options, debt and equity, all around, but it serves an illustrative purpose and shapes a perspective that can at least be thought about. If the premise is subsequently modified, augmented, even negated, so be it, at least we begin somewhere and go forth.

So, from the top... The asset of a business is here defined as its fundamental and dependable core, that which generates dependable and fundamental value. In some cases this comprises more or less predictable cash flows, a more or less predictable liquidation value, a more or less replaceable presence in some more or less predictable market. In short, the asset is predicated on some level of predictability, and for this reason it can be financed with more or less security. The option, on the other hand, is unpredictable. It is the potential, the opportunity, as it were, some of which is imagined and some not even – certainty approaching nil.

Because the delineation is not always as straight-forward as is implied here, enterprise is financed in ways that are not always straight-forward and the market often sets values in seemingly fickle ways. For instance, the liquidation preference set by a venture investor seeks to capture some downside protection and to isolate the asset from the option in a startup (which is essentially all optionality). From the issuer's perspective, the structure is a form of financial leverage, subordinating other financial interests in the same way that a mortgage subordinates the homeowner's equity.

These variations are set in arbitrary ways, because both the asset and the option are ultimately in the eye of the beholder. A founder probably considers the optionality of his or her business to be a true asset, just as a homeowner adores the sculpted plate on top of the doorway more jealously than the couple passing through with their broker. That's when negotiation happens, and that's when market standards are applied, because presumably both the startup founder and the homeowner can get his or her asset and option more fully valued elsewhere if need be. By the same token, this is where markets have been known to create excesses.

For instance, the debt markets – which for a long time had been based on a borrower's ability to support a loan through the value generated by a certain asset – have become increasingly linked to refinance (as distinct from repayment) and hedged churn (as distinct from holding to maturity). There is valid support for this trend in markets that are always more sophisticated and fluid, but the theme smacks a little bit of optionality financed as an asset, of potential financed as a given. (That bubble popped once, in the sub-prime mortgage devastation, and there are always stirrings happening in other markets, which may lead some to reminisce.) By the same token, if secondary private dealing had overpriced Facebook ahead of the company's IPO, this was a speculative trade that valued the optionality of the underlying business to a point of excess and overestimated the broader market's willingness to do the same.

The common thread in all of the extracted samples – from the venture funding to the homeowner's equity to the sub-prime crisis to the Facebook IPO – is the suggestion that optionality and true asset finance are sometimes mixed up, and that the valuations that are set sometimes reflect the confusion. When investments are predicated on trade, takeout, rollover, exit, and other assorted synonyms that more or less mean the same thing, such decisions are largely based on speculation about market sentiment, liquidity, and continuity. This is optionality, not asset, and the risk is equity risk, not debt. Investors have at times been prone to misprice the situation, and founders have at times been prone to lose sight. In an era of business and financial convergence, this really stands to reason.

3. When technical is fundamental

When the markets peaked around 2007 and 2008, there was a pervasive approach to investments – in every segment from corporate fixed income to consumer credit to equities – that was predicated on refinancing risk rather than repayment capacity, on exits rather than interim cash flows. In this manner of making capital allocation decisions, the analysis of capital flows and market liquidity is of equal (or greater) importance to an appraisal of the underlying asset that is being financed. The bet is on an escape valve, a handoff, in an ongoing flow of ownership or credit. In such a scenario invested capital is permanent and financial holdings are rented rather than owned, if you will. Here, "technical" analysis is as (or more) fundamental as (than) "fundamental" analysis itself.

There is an interesting analogy that we can look to, that for the last fifteen years or so has also been driven by liquidity, at multiple stages of the cycle, and has seen its share of ebbs and flows for that same reason. This asset class has also for the most part relied on refinancing or replacement, rather than the cash flows of an underlying business: venture capital.

In venture investing, the underlying property has little fundamental value at the time of entry. The value mainly lies in the option, and the realization of value is in the trade: the follow-on round, the IPO, the M&A event. A notable aspect of this analogy is the almost circular system that includes the public markets, the universe of M&A alternatives, and venture capital. Each one is influenced by and in turn influences the others, and to the extent that a bubble pops in one, the others suffer the effects and in ways could be the cause.

This circularity and codependence have always been the case and do not in themselves signify a new development, but the novelty of today's landscape is in the convergence of investment categories and styles. While different segments of the capital markets could in the past be distinguished by differences in approach to risk, which differences served as a balancing mechanism of sorts, this may become less true in a market largely (almost purely) driven by optionality, and one in which liquidity and handoff is not only a possibility (as second way out) but an expected outcome.

4. An entrepreneur's guide to the trading desk

Earnings season is always an exciting time to watch markets, even if only for entertainment value. Financial gamesmanship seems always to escalate, or at least manifest itself more visibly, when companies announce their quarterly results. There is not only the bilateral dynamic between guidance and actual postings – a delicate balance – but the triangular relationship between guidance and results and market expectations. The market, after all, makes its own assumptions and has three months between seasons to fine tune and adjust. In regard to expectations, furthermore, there is the interplay between analyst consensus and whisper number, and all this before we even get into systemic factors that push values up or down regardless of a company's performance.

Entertainment value aside, interpreting (or at least monitoring) these gyrations, convolutions, relationships and inconsistencies in the public markets, can be important for those outside of the daily trade. For starters, there is an inherent statement in the markets about the broader economic environment and its prospects. But another and maybe even more critical reason to monitor the flow is to glean insights this provides into the funding environment, for which the public market often serves as a guide. It isn't only that private valuations are informed by public metrics, but that the very consummation of private transactions is influenced by the health of public holdings and assets represented thereby. When, back in 2008 and 2009, public stocks had fallen, M&A as well as private investing came to a relative halt. For strategic buyers this had a lot to do with loss of confidence, which relates back to economic aspects (as previously described). For financial investors, this was the result of collapsing portfolio values, the math of which improved considerably in ensuing periods.

Among founders and other entrepreneurs, the topics raised have not been common in discussions, focused as business builders rightly should be on building businesses. These subjects, however, and business building, are closely connected, if not overlapped, and should take up a great and growing share of entrepreneurial thinking. Operations, growth strategies, product launches, customer interaction, and others aspects of successful enterprise being determined by economic conditions, and all such aspects requiring planning prior to implementation, economic advance notice should be much appreciated. The earlier and more complete the notice, the more effective the plan and its implementation. Although markets are fickle and sometimes anticipate but otherwise trail economic (and industry) patterns, thoughtful reading of market conditions will only complete a picture that couldn't ever be too detailed.

As importantly, maybe more so, there is the aspect of corporate finance. Some businesses are never done raising capital, some investors are never done selling shares, and certain securities can never be finished rolling over. Even limiting this discussion to the primary private market, certain correspondences stand out. For example, public stocks began their never-ending rebound from the depths of panic right around the time that massive liquidity through quantitative easing was introduced, and introduced some more. This path had also coincided with the advent of what some now refer back to as a seed and late-stage venture bubble. It wasn't the bubble per se but the unevenness of it that would have profoundly impacted business ventures as these expanded.

One starting a business, or one continuing to build an enterprise, should pay close attention to these issues, as these will determine the future to at least the same extent as the quality of a given product or a business model. While it is critical to think in terms of sector trends and venture motifs, for obvious reasons, it is as important to be versed in the more esoteric: Inflation and deflation, quantitative easing and its impact, employment growth and ways that this is measured, the flows that push financial markets daily, and those that could cause directions to reverse.

For startup founders it wasn't always so, but when the distinctions start to fade between technical and fundamental, early and late, private and public, so also the neat homework assignments for the class will start to flow over into the next semester's curriculum, or the lecture in the room next door.

5. The next phase to old finance for new media

All capital is bridge capital and all funding needs to be repaid. The distinctions between equity and debt finance, between terms (long- and short-), between cash flow and assets, between internal or external liquidity sources, are mainly matters of degree. Ultimately the underlying business must perform and the assets must produce cash. At least at some point. And at least sufficiently so to justify financing, which must be returned. Whether through business cash flow or market liquidity – itself linked to the underlying business – funds are returned or else written off. The question is really about when, how, and how much.

In these nuances and degrees, one of the traditional differentiators between debt and equity has had to do with theoretical term and theoretical repayment source. Debt in theory has a shorter term than equity, which is in theory permanent capital, and debt is in theory repaid whereas equity is sold. As a result of these differences, and one important other to which we'll come back, debt is less expensive than equity for a business. Because of the other difference, that is a legal obligation and priority claim on assets, debt also comes with higher risk for the borrower, and thus financial leverage is, in theory, taken seriously.

But the subject is murky and getting murkier, because theory and practice are often quite different in nature. As capital markets have become more liquid a great deal of corporate debt is not lent as much as underwritten and traded, and borrowers often don't repay as much as they refinance. By the same token, at least in certain investment categories, some equity has preferential rank over business liquidity in relation to other capital tiers, and this has become particularly notable in the latest era of venture capital and technology startups.

It is this latter segment that brings us to the true subject of this essay. Taking the assortment of themes discussed and stirring them up in a salad mix on top of which we add the dressing of a segment becoming more mature, we derive a dish that hints of an increasing debt profile, debt opportunity, and debt finance activity. This is at the tail end of an era that began with the purest form of equity and equity-risk that there is: venture-stage funding for businesses with no assets and no profit. These businesses have grown, the asset base has developed, the profit picture is coming into focus, and markets have evolved.

For digital media and its related technology and service platforms, the next stage in the series of financial bridges is more and more likely to be a move up the capital structure. It is more and more likely to be an acceptance of credit risk and lower price by both borrowers and investors, eventually leading back to the ways in which media has traditionally been financed – with a blend of debt and equity against assets and cash flows of substance. This has already begun to happen at the largest and most credit-worthy levels of the sector, and at the smallest and most speculative, where credit and venture funding can be almost synonymous for founders and their early backers.

6. Creative finance in the middle stage

The scenario goes something like this. A company is several years old, and has been a reasonable success in the consumer web. This is to say, its app is used with greater or lesser regularity. The company has a presence, in other words, and gathers data that now needs to be monetized. In short, its presence has not yet been turned into a business, but perhaps it can be. This company is at a crossroads, not unusual for a free consumer web where users have gotten used to free product. But business is still business and costs must be covered.

In this scenario we see a company with value, possibly quite large, that cannot be fully understood. There is value in its utility, in its data, in its back-end technology and analytics, in its front-end design and consumer recognition, but absent cash flows what does that value really mean, and to whom. No question mark there because the question is rhetorical. We don't know, and maybe not even its venture backers do, who have watched the company evolve and supported it with sizable investments, let's say $70 million just to pick a number. Years and millions later, the crossroads. Not unusual.

The scenario plays out in this fashion all the time, and necessarily must, because any business constructed on no charge eventually gets to that point. Even a business constructed on some charge that's insufficient to cover the base, or a business built on some future charge that will be sufficient at that time, these are all merely matters of degree. The success or failure of any such venture is determined by some element of unknown possibility and its capitalization contains some element of option value. That is the crossroads. When that option gets exercised, the value is locked in, and the choice at the intersection is made. Right or left.

We often see these intersections with their options and unanswered questions at very early stages of business building. For this reason, seed-stage financings are frequently consummated as convertible notes, postponing the valuation discussion to a point where the choice at the crossroads is more likely to be made. (That is arguably the Series A funding event, although a so-called Series A crunch tells us that many such businesses are not ready for the option exercise just yet.) Then tougher decisions happen, or are postponed again, as the case may be. And sometimes it turns out that the decision was premature.

When, say, $70 million has been raised and valuations have been set, in theory the directional choice at the intersection was made. But in actuality the crossroads we thought we passed might have been jumping the gun. It happens, and there are ways to remedy the mishap with corporate finance. This used to be called a "down round," which was like taking steps back to the original intersection, but that was before markets had fully thought through the breaking up of value into component pieces: There is the existing asset, and there is the optionality. It isn't all one, and it does not have to be reflected as an all or nothing proposition.

One can instead go back in time, which is to say, reset the option by funding the isolated asset and gaining leeway – without resetting the full enterprise valuation. One can, for instance, borrow some amount of senior debt, say something less than $40 million, that will in a downside scenario – that is, a scenario in which the optionality doesn't materialize – get adequate coverage from the asset. In this example, if $70 million has built a recognized platform with utility and lots of data and analytics and consumer presence, perhaps fifty cents on the dollar (give or take) isn't a bad coverage ratio.

For equity owners this does several things. It allows new outside capital to come in without painful valuation discussions; it extends and leverages the optionality of the initial investment; and it keeps management's feet to the same fire without a reset of stock options and targets that might have accompanied a revaluation of the enterprise. For management the runway is not insubstantial, what with the head start that the first $70 million has provided already. Which said, however, the downside of the structure is the downside of any leveraged deal. If the asset doesn't grow into its option value, priority claims are priority claims, and borrowing turns messy. At any stage.

7. Hyper-ubiquity, cont'd

In short, some things are different now. The list of these things is long (and getting longer even as I write), but we focus on things in capital markets for simplicity. More precisely, this is about capital markets for media and information technology, and businesses in and around that echo chamber. There used to be a clear distinction between old and new media, and between hardware and software, and between various categories within the digital media universe – for instance, information, entertainment, and social media; or advertising and direct commerce. There was a clear distinction between early- and mid-stage and mature ventures, and with such distinctions asset classes and investment styles were also distinct. Some of these things are different now.

There is a disappearing now of many such differences. The segments and sub-segments are combining, the business-cycle stages are less obvious, and the financing structures are less cut-and-dry. It's natural that this should be the case as the underlying industry is transitioning from what was a clear beginning – born from personal computing, the Internet, and mobility – to a point of maturation that hasn't quite yet arrived (and possibly never will). In beginnings, assets are clearly venture-stage; at maturation these are for private equity or debt capital or strategic buyout. In times of transition from one to the other, the financing structure is somewhere between, and not quite either one. (We leave out the IPO market from this discussion – which has not been much of a market in the period in question anyway – but mainly for purposes of simplicity.)

The topic of sector overlap has been covered in these pages extensively. The present installment – in continuation of its precursors in this section of the book – is more properly related to financial flows and structures. (But it is difficult to draw a demarcation line where the sector dynamic ends and financial consequence commences.) No matter, the core idea for present purposes is this: When the business cycle is at a cut-and-dry stage, whether purely new or perfectly mature, finance specialization and classification falls naturally into place; but when there is transition, and especially when it is two-dimensional – by business cycle and also by business profile (in an environment of convergence as described) – financial hyperspecialty is limiting and in ways suboptimal.

In the financial press news always draws attention lately to an emerging overlap in financial asset class, investment appetite, and deal structure. Here is a venture-backed company doing a leveraged recap privately (in lieu of an IPO) with debt from a major bank and equity from a venture-active strategic investor and global hedge fund. Here is a bootstrapped 18-year old company that raised its first capital from a mixed syndicate of venture- and later-stage private equity sources. Here is a large-cap public company in the consumer hardware segment, seeking (unusually) to go private through a leveraged buyout. Here is a Series C venture round led by a small specialized fund that's been historically associated with seed and Series A financing.

There is a picture that comes into focus in this hodgepodge of categories and structures, and the picture is the mix itself. Sometimes financial markets determine the themes of industry and sometimes markets react to trends already underway. On one or two levels, when patterns solidify to become ubiquitously real, the distinction doesn't matter.

8. To the rebirth of efficient markets

The order often can't be filled. This isn't because of anything poorly conceived about the order, but something limiting about the place, the time, the circumstance, the market. Some projects, certain funds, particular profiles, simply do not fit the mold that's offered. One venture requires too much, another requires too little. One sector is in vogue, another is ahead or behind it. One public stock doesn't trade, another shouldn't be public. One funding source needs short-term lift, while another needs long-term gestation. These issues and others are wholly external to the quality presented by issuers, borrowers, sellers, fundraisers. But these are all variables that frequently cause orders to go unfilled. It isn't the asset, but how it fits the formula.

One might imagine a time when finance wasn't exactly this way. There was perhaps a time when finance structures, returns, and liquidity were more properly a continuum, part of a flow rather than patterns of rigid boxes that are often detached and scattered. The difference is analogous to interpreted nuance versus binary code, priced flexibility versus determined step-functions, the "here's how" versus simplistic "yes/no" responses. One can surmise some things from history – say, the original merchant bankers – and envision transactions completed in a more analog fashion than the engineered structures described. One might surmise this from the very nature of finance theory – the capital asset pricing model, modern portfolio theory, and the like – which sciences are based on a widely populated, multi-varied market. The resulting graphs are steady rather than broken lines, and the shapes are curved rather than angular.

If there has been a change in atmosphere, perhaps this is related to an increasingly consolidated and institutional environment, and a set of realities that reflect it. Whether public or private, early-stage or late, equity or debt, fund-structured or banked, the pools of capital are bigger and require bigger absolute returns. The professionally managed portfolios are defined by strict categories and investment strategies, so that other institutions can in turn click the right box on the checklist. Asset classes are tightly scoped in order to be packaged, processed, sometimes sold off. In theory, this sort of environment would suggest enhanced liquidity and efficiency, but in reality this is limited to confined zones only, and these have been known to change, sometimes abruptly.

In this sort of environment, opportunities can get lost – as already said, not necessarily due to their intrinsic nature, but because they don't fit the mold, which mold may be a different mold presently than even a short time hence.

But there is help on the way, and it is due to the described environment precisely that it is coming. Increased sophistication and technical advances reflected in several decades of financial innovation are giving rise to freer information flow and more efficient and accessible processing.

Central to and at the very core of markets, information begets capital and the freer the flow of both the greater a market's efficiency. When a greater cross-section of investors can participate, a greater assortment of issuers can find liquidity. We are still only at the beginning of the movement – characterized by peer-to-peer finance, online research and transaction access, innovative payment and processing platforms, all aided and abetted by social networks – but it is important for the movement to continue and gain momentum.

When some market observers hear of democratization and fragmentation in finance, they shudder. This is based on a perception that money is being protected more skillfully in concentrated pockets. This, as we have learned, is false. The most important contributor to financial health is an efficient market, which is a market involving many rather than few, and the most important contributor to economic wellbeing is a market in which deserving projects are funded and priced in accordance to their inherent merit, rather than financial trend and the whims of concentrated trendsetters. A market of one is not a true market, and capital pricing in it may or may not reflect the risk.

We should not shudder at the thought of market fragmentation, we should welcome this and encourage its peaceful evolution.

9. The limits of hyper-data and the limits of efficiency

Is there a point at which information processing is so rapid and complete that capital markets could as a result become less (rather than more) efficient? It would seem, on the contrary, that the more quickly, the more comprehensively, investors can act upon new information, the more efficient the market pricing mechanism becomes. But this perspective has not been fully tested in an environment in which massive quantities of global data can be factored into execution virtually instantly, and in massive sums.

As data processing taps into its vast potential with new tools and systems to facilitate pattern recognition and other hyper-intelligence in consumer behavior, economic forecasting, and capital flows, a new competitive criterion is emerging in the financial sector: the ability to absorb and utilize the most available data the fastest. Taken to an extreme, a concentration of "brainpower," lacking a better term, is in the case of markets not dissimilar to a concentration of capital.

We have seen (and in the prior chapter touched upon) what may be the result of fund flows that are pushed and prodded by concentrated pools. In theory, a market is most efficient when there is a fragmented base of participants with diverse perspectives. By extension, as such diversity diminishes, efficiency becomes less perfect. In an extreme case – a market of one (or, more plausibly, a completely unified market) – the theoretical inefficiency is total.

Now, is it possible that what is true for capital concentration is also true for information concentration? If a narrow group should come to dominate information processing in the manner described, would this not similarly result in a reduction of market diversity? Would such an environment not encourage those less "informed" to emulate the trading of investors "in the know," resulting in even more concentrated centers of influence? (As a reminder, we might look at rating agencies and their role in the debt bubble and burst a few years ago. New information bases are beginning to emerge, which are not rating agencies per se but on a certain level may serve a similar market function, wittingly or not.)

The questions are conceptual, and lead to other conceptual questions. But with the data movement well underway, the currently conceptual might take on more practical undertones shortly. At a sufficiently high level, capital and information become synonymous. Much of the analysis presented leads to this conclusion.

10. Crowds and flows

The term crowdfunding is sensationally deceiving. The intended significance of it – that businesses, projects, even individuals, can access financing from a crowd – in actuality describes traditional markets and banking. Crowds deposit funds into banks, and banks use these deposits to make loans to businesses and projects, and crowds. Insurance companies use funds contributed by their collective of policy holders to invest in debt obligations. These institutions and others (such as university endowments, for instance, which receive funding from crowds of alumni) also invest in hedge funds and private equity and venture capital pools, which crowd around stocks or certain startups.

One difference between crowdfunding in its intended sense and the mechanic of traditional markets is that of intermediation. There is a directness implied in crowdfunding that does away with the crowd of managers and general partners and officers of funds and banks and the like. This is referred to as *disintermediation*, which is also sensationally deceiving. It's just that a new batch of intermediaries emerges to replace the old. Instead of Bailey Savings & Loan and Duke & Duke there are now Lending Club and AngelList and the like, or rather there is all of the above, at least for now. The sources of finance – the crowd, in the abstract – is only driven through different (or added) filters, which is intermediation all the same.

A truer difference between crowdfunding and traditional market mechanics is perhaps one of consciousness. Bank depositors don't think about the mortgage and small business loans transacted with their savings, but actively participate in the process known as crowdfunding. In the same sense, an individual's insurance or pension plan might run through a chain of redirections and advances to eventually end up as a tiny fraction of Twitter's IPO, or this individual could consciously throw in a buck or two into the next Twitter through FundersClub. In any of these cases decisions occur somehow, somewhere, maybe at different levels and in different numbers. The crowd all the same is a presence, more or less active, more or less conscious.

Consciousness and vocal participation, however, is a critical distinction in the case of crowds. It is especially so in an era of many voices that make themselves heard through social media outlets. Through these bullhorns messages carry farther and crowds can be more effectively stirred up. When crowds get excessively stirred we sometimes have what is known in traditional markets as a *bubble*, or, more delicately, *momentum*. Sometimes the crowd dissipates, and the bubble pops. If and when the crowd comes back there is volatility. And sometimes these waves are idea bubbles – traditionally known as *groupthink*, or, more delicately, *style* – that can also dissolve and pop like an inflated stock.

Studying crowd behavior isn't limited to markets, (although many things that aren't about money flows really are). Stadiums filled with cheering fans, the rhythmic motion of a concert crowd, the traffic patterns of cars and pedestrians around the midtown area during holidays, these all share some common characteristics. By the same token, *likes* and *retweets* are momentum patterns in a crowd of followers, and these aren't the only ways in which markets and media overlap. Increasingly, really, it's one and the same.

Although studying crowd behavior isn't new, it warrants a renewal for some of us in this new context of the popular web, crowdfunding, and marketplaces. *Crowds and Power* is the title of a 1960 publication by Elias Canetti, who won the Nobel Prize in 1981. Its subject is the observation of crowd patterns in a variety of historical and then-current circumstances, analyzed from the perspective of psychology, art, politics, physical movement, expansion, diminution, and other related variables that, taken literally, have to do with public demonstrations and the rise or fall of social collectives. Taken figuratively, however, there are fascinating similarities between such traditional crowds and newer, more virtual ones, and between the concentrations and dispersals of past movements and more modern ones – say, the alternative currency phenomenon known as Bitcoin.

The contrarian approach isn't always right, the opportunity isn't always greatest where the crowd isn't. To know the distinction, one may as well begin by understanding the subject.

11. The interconnection of market currents

Ripples in the M&A market cause waves to happen in private equity. Performances of IPOs determine outlooks in venture capital. All of these things impact the way executives and other entrepreneurs make decisions. Some of these decision makers are angel investors, and they influence the way founders found. Some of these founders are M&A or IPO survivors, some seek and others provide new money. The private equity and venture capital communities ebb and flow with the results. It is impossible to assess any one of these elements in isolation. Each is a piece of and in turn shapes the whole.

In another chapter here the notion of universal specialization is dealt with in the context of overlapping industry segments and converging technology themes. But this doesn't go far enough. There is the capital to consider, and its moods, as described. There are the structural aspects of liquidity, and possibilities that these open or close. There is as well the impact of new technologies upon the very modes of finance that underpin them. The funding and operation are connected. Although the manner of association is varied, the link is impossible to break. Even along new paths, basic finance rules are inescapable. A few of these were touched upon in prior (and next) chapters here.

12. Technology, profit and network effect

There is a conflict in theoretical finance between technology evolution (obsolescence) on one hand, and the concept of perpetuity (ongoing concern) on the other. In theory, business appraisal is based on a series of cash flows capped off by a terminal value, reflecting an enterprise profile extended into an indeterminate horizon. In reality, the modern enterprise does not lend itself to such easy extension. What, for example, was the forecasted terminal value of the telephone company twenty-five years ago, and what can it be for the wireless carrier today? How confident did we feel then, and how confident do we feel now in pinning down an exit multiple, or in determining the cash flow profile on which to base it? How can we know the line of work of, say, a broadcaster in five years' time? When we take in Amazon and WalMart in the same picture, which one do we see as most likely to compete with Facebook, and exactly how? And how likely is it that Facebook's evolving platform will displace Google's, or Groupon's, or both, or neither?

It is a question of relativity, I suppose. IBM the typewriter company may in its day have been as difficult to appraise as our contemporaries, but the foreseeable future then was (at least according to nostalgia) more robust than it has become. In the long term, then and now, everyone is... you know... but the long term is now the least of our worries. When two-year old companies are transforming retail and retail is transforming entertainment and entertainment is driven by social media, which is driven by perpetual innovation, our financial models fall apart beyond Year One. From a valuation perspective, the rapid-fire transformations imply that equity value, more than ever, is really option value. We invest in order to be in the game, so to speak, and in our assessments the best we can often do is try to avoid clear mistakes, focus on certain themes, try not to miscalculate the markets, and follow guideposts with some degree of flexibility.

In connected systems, which encompasses a great deal, one set of guideposts that we can navigate by – there are several – are the following value drivers and pillars of differentiation: technology, profit, network effect; not necessarily all three, and not necessarily in that order. As we look at the sector holistically, as we try to the best of our ability to sift through the distractions, unpredictability, and option value disguised as equity, these three areas of strength may be as close to a permanent rule as we will likely encounter.

New Labor & New Capital

1. Investors in a portfolio of one

Venture investing and entrepreneurship are two sides of the same coin, at least from the entrepreneur's side of it. According to one definition of the word *entrepreneur*, this is a person who "has possession of a new enterprise, venture or idea and is accountable for its inherent risks and outcome." Note the presence of terms such as venture and risk in the definition. Note the root derivation from enterprise and its possession. These are words that could just as well be found in descriptions of investing and its aspects. There is, however, a difference of diversification, in that an entrepreneur is usually invested in a portfolio of one, and is exposed completely to its success. Investors, in the pure sense, will spread their bets, and are by the same token less accountable.

In the dance between the two – the ritual of raising capital in support of building an enterprise – the entrepreneur often takes the investor's lead. But in fairness as well as common sense, it should not be so. According to the definitional analysis above, the risk and responsibility weighs much more heavily with the entrepreneur, for which reason alone he or she should be the more credible party. Nevertheless… entrepreneurs need capital and investors have it… so it goes. And therefore, again, the way investors go so do entrepreneurs, very often. The theme is particularly pronounced where one investor's (or group's) capital is the only capital, at least for a while; where revenues (let alone cash flows) are prone to lie somewhere along the proverbial horizon – which dreamscape may be more distant in certain ventures than others.

As one qualifies the distinction between an entrepreneur and an investor by defining the entrepreneur as a wholly un-diversified investor who must often follow the lead of others who have much less at risk but sometimes take confident liberties from their position of strength, it may serve some well to guard against recklessness. If offered a choice, advice (and capital) from those with the narrowest diversification and the most at risk is, in one sense, best. We find, maybe not surprisingly, this leads directly to customers: the best and truest advisors and capital providers.

2. In a diverse portfolio of mispriced options

Entrepreneurs sell equity, venture capitalists buy options. This explains so much of what has, in some circles, been a mutual disgruntlement.

It has been commonplace among many, entrepreneurs and investors alike, to beat up on the venture model – in blogs, on websites, in discussion panels – so frequent and oft-quoted that I won't even bother to cite specifics. Entrepreneurs complain about control, about investors' unconcern for founders, about the VC's push or resistance to exit, about liquidation preferences, and so much more. Investors and their close observers complain about the economics, and stretching to make these work when hit rates in the startup realm are low.

But no wonder, really. How can economics be compelling when the asset is from the outset mispriced, when options are acquired for full enterprise value, or even higher? How can entrepreneurs expect venture investors to relax when the margin for error is less than very slim? Would any hedge fund buy a tech stock's calls for the full underlying stock price? Would anyone pay this for the right to buy the very same stock at the same price or higher later on?

This is in many ways what venture investing is – even outside of systemic waves and massive flows that have for decades propped and raised the levels of liquidity, and increased competition and purchase prices. The VC writes a check knowing that the business will, almost by definition, become a different business altogether before it's time to write a second. Worse, nobody, not even the entrepreneur, knows what that future business will be. The option might soon just expire.

So when VCs buy these expensive options, how can they not be sensitive about them? How can they not insist on liquidation preferences and not be finicky about the exit? As well, how can entrepreneurs who have sold such fully priced options not expect to be monitored and watched and structured and prodded?

Now, where does the line get drawn between a venture and a tech stock, when their respective futures are almost equally unknown?

3. Arendt's ingredients of enterprise

As a disenchanted philosopher, still early in her career, Hannah Arendt redirected her attention to *activity*. As a philosopher nevertheless, at heart and in her training, she conducted the study of activity with an erudite and historical eye, practiced in the organizing, discerning, analytic methods of her discipline's forebears. The result was a series of essays in which activity is deconstructed, reconstructed, distilled, cleansed of redundancy and distortion, and laid bare in its purest and most practical form. In short, Hannah Arendt was – among other qualities and maybe unconsciously – a teacher of enterprise, who has contributed important ideas to the field and can be studied by its participants with gain.

To abbreviate some of her investigations and conclusions, the "active life" – which for purposes of this article we can think of as the life in enterprise – consists of three distinct sub-compartments of activity, so to speak, each one unique and serving a special function, but complementary to the others and necessary to the whole. In order, these are (1) labor, (2) work, and (3) action. *Labor* refers to a body's mechanism of self-preservation and growth, which in its literal sense is of a biological nature. *Work* is the set of more deliberate acts performed by the individual (or group) in order to produce new forms, new objects, new solutions or ideas. Neither labor nor work, however, presupposes a societal collective, and this is how *action* completes the picture – it being a type of activity that connects individuals or groups with other individuals, groups or things.

In the realm of the enterprise, clear parallels can be recognized. Labor, for example, can be seen as the internal development and safeguarding of the business mechanism – its organization, resources, and terrain. Work is the production – technical or otherwise – of whatever it is that the business offers to its customers. Action, finally, is the commerce – the customer contact, competitive dynamic, and other facets of business association within the marketplace. As these elements of activity interrelate and coexist in the enterprise, they each require a very particular set of talents and very unique preparation. What's more, any business that does not bring together all three ingredients, as described, is not truly a business, but more likely, perhaps, a product, a feature, or worse still, a hobby.

To many, the ideas reflected herein will seem like a restatement of the obvious, but maybe there are aspects of obviousness and restatement in all philosophy. That Arendt's thesis was moreover not meant as specifically instructional for entrepreneurs – narrowly defined – should not cause entrepreneurs to see this discussion as misplaced, because almost everyone is an entrepreneur, at least by analogy.

Nor should it be distracting for any who go from here to the source material, that Arendt's illustrative examples are drawn from among the ancients, such as the Roman generals and Greek politicians, who were clearly out of tune with the futuristic reality that would eventually unfold. Such universality is exactly the value of classics, like Hannah Arendt's and her predecessors': The "obvious" that they convey only seems so once it is revealed, and the lessons of the ancients are more timeless than we sometimes realize.

4. From speculation to personal equity

I see an interesting new theme emerging. It makes for a refreshing incidence and welcome new approach. Lacking a better term, let's call this an investment thesis focused on the self: learning, work, expertise building; in short, an investment in personal equity.

For instance, a leading tech investor – an entrepreneur and student of the trade – has urged his followers to stay away from speculation, to preserve capital and invest to "[become] knowledgeable about the business of something [they] really love to do." While on the surface unrelated, at roughly that same time a high-profile venture syndicate funded a social teaching startup, the mission of which is to "transform every community into a campus, every address into a classroom, and every neighbor into a teacher and student." In the meantime, one of the leading textbook rental companies has announced its acquisition of an online tutoring firm, while new web services are always rolling out to teach coding skills to would-be programmers and other skills to would-be others.

The positions and activities described would have been welcome in any market, symbolic as these are of dedication, hard work and self-improvement (as distinct from speculation and myopic financial motive). That the noted theme of personal value- and substance-building happens to coincide with a time when speculation had turned on itself in ways more or less destructive should not be taken as ironic.

As already said, it is a welcome theme and a refreshing approach that should be taken seriously and imitated when possible. That it may perhaps be more convenient to do so nowadays than it was when other options more generously beckoned, this also is not a silver lining to overlook for all the gray around it.

If global change and some disorientation have served as catalyst for a positive inward dedication, for a longer-term commitment to growth and personal value creation, then so be it and let us be thankful for confusion. But, within reason, within reason... maybe needlessly to say.

Excess is never good, in any variety. We must hope that the inward reorientation as well as external tumult from which it arguably stems, don't go too far and coincide too perfectly.

5. Of employees, partners, profits and progress

The profit motive is getting a bum rap in some circles. The subject is complicated, and like other complicated subjects lends itself to deceptive simplification. Most recently it has been argued that corporate profit and business progress are incompatible; or rather, that the method behind short-term profit optimization is incompatible with long-term innovation, because earnings and value are not at all times in sync and the formulas for measuring value and potential are thus misguided. As high-reaching as the argument has been, it is not new, and it only scratches the surface of where more fundamental fault lines are buried.

The tension between short-term earnings and the investment necessary to develop long-term value has always been at the core of executive decision-making. The tools devised by academia to push this process along – internal rate of return, return on capital, discounted cash flow – each have had greater or lesser merit depending on circumstance. To attack the tools or the desire for profit is to miss the point of enterprise and to confuse results with causes. If future value is sacrificed to immediate earnings, if innovation is stifled by reluctance to take risk, or, by the same token, if inordinate risk is taken today at the expense of tomorrow's value, neither the analysis nor the drive for profit is to blame. The cause, rather, is in the frame of mind, the basis from which strategies form and are implemented.

As has been argued in some circles, the Wall Street model may have suffered some when banking firms stopped being partnerships. Several aspects of partnership (and partnership only) are conducive to a balanced view of risk and reward, in the near-term and the long.

There is ownership and pride in building what one owns, there is stability in one's role, and there is one's own capital at risk. Arguably, when Wall Street firms went public, the features that had made these firms most successful (and special) diminished. Ownership became fragmented at best, and certainly marginalized; individual reward got tied to immediate revenue; and individual expposure was reduced through disassociation from losses and cash payouts that were connected to near-term gain. In short, partners became employees. And the same issues carry through far beyond Wall Street into the broader industrial base.

Returning now to the original arguments presented above – about profit and innovation in counterbalance, about near-term sacrifice and long-term value, about financial formula as a tool that may not capture the true worth of invention – these all have to be taken in perspective. These should be considered in the context of decisions made by deciders – rather than decisions made by circuitry and spreadsheets – and deciders are motivated as human beings are.

We are all marked by mood and whims and diversity of taste, we are all to a greater or lesser extent self absorbed, we all think we own certain things and wish we owned others.

Ownership, in the last analysis, is its own profit and loss, and innovation.

6. Advertiser turned marketer and consumer turned vendor

There was a time when media at least put on a pretense of distributing content that was of intrinsic value, independent of the advertising that enveloped it. And because this advertising was not immediately actionable, there was between the consumer's wallet and the vendor a chain of reactions, stimuli and responses, all of which served as a sort of buffer between the message and the point of purchase. This buffer, and its corresponding passage of time, was filled with (among other things) content: television programming, magazine articles, radio DJ personalities and their shows.

But such cozy consumerism days are leaving us fast, in fact may be far gone already, and in the place of advertising we now see marketing stepping in and taking charge. The distinction is one of process to a closing. Where advertising suggests – the features of a brand, the address of a destination – marketing requests the credit card number. Where advertising plants seeds, marketing seeks to harvest.

The television infomercials may be a result or a cause, who knows, but it can't be coincidental that these began to take over the TV screens in living rooms at around the same time that Internet usage expanded in the office. The impulse buying behavior is similar in both cases, and the toll free number to call for the sharpest-ever razor blade is just another mouse-click for some online purchase.

In such an environment, the delicate ways of creative advertising and public relations are being supplanted by the more aggressive modes of programmatic placements. Similarly, impression-based CPM is moving in the direction of success rather than guesswork – cost-per-click (CPC) and cost-per-action (CPA) – and what we thought was an innocent tweet from a friend about the mystery thriller that he or she is enjoying, may in fact be an e-commerce campaign for Amazon.com.

As advertising thus migrates to the faster and more direct pace of marketing, the line between entertainment and commerce gets erased, and the difference between media and consumer retail vanishes. Simultaneously, as the primary connection device shifts from the local airwaves to the web, the marketing opportunity expands beyond the local market and to the world, and the cost and ease of marketing to a large audience diminishes: Yes, anyone can now be a vendor.

When Amazon initiated a user-driven social media-based marketing program, this marked an important milestone in the evolution of the consumer economy. Rather than a market fueled by consumer spending, this could be the beginning of one based on consumer vending, in which millions of impulse shoppers become millions of little marketers. Somehow I feel Google stands to gain from this.

7. The R&D department or the bank

In other news, inflation is no longer of concern. Analysts have written extensively about the impact on stock markets and broader financial environment of a low- or dis-inflation environment. There has also been much commentary about a separate phenomenon – not unrelated – which is our jobless "recovery." The case has been argued that small businesses and entrepreneurship can go a long way to boost employment and economic productivity. What we have not seen, or at least not with the same degree of attention, is commentary that combines the concepts – assessing the potential impact of no inflation or even deflation upon entrepreneurship and small business. As the situation becomes more pronounced, the subject should warrant scrutiny.

The digital media and technology sectors, which have been a breeding ground for entrepreneurship for much more than a decade, comprise an interesting laboratory in which to observe such issues. And as this segment contains some of the world's largest and most successful corporations, the actions of its participants can provide useful insights to entrepreneurs as they seek, as always, to navigate uncharted terrain. Because the Internet and many of its affiliated segments – e-commerce, devices, communication services and infrastructure – have been marked by deflationary economics for a long time, the activities of this sector's participants really are exemplary of a deflationary economy, and serve as a useful case study.

Some initial observations follow. As indicated, these are based largely and as a matter of convenience on the digital media and technology sectors, where examples in support of each presented comment are numerous. Nevertheless, this is only a superficial look and is not meant to be more than that. Many of the notes are basic, and others are intuitive. Not all are obvious. It is anyway interesting to frame what we may already perceive into a current economic subtext, from which starting-point roadmaps may be charted.

(1) To set the stage, a precept: Within a range of financial asset classes, with cash at one extreme and equities at the other, a high-inflation environment favors equities over cash, and a deflationary environment will reflect the opposite preference. Other forms of capital (between the two extremes) vary in accordance to their proximity to cash or stocks.

(2) In a period of negligible inflation or deflation, cash will gain favor with investors, relative to stocks, and the extent of the dis-inflation will determine the degree to which cash is preferred.

(3) In very broad terms, companies accumulate cash – or pay down debt, which is a corollary – as a means to prop up equity with a floor underneath its value.

(4) In very broad terms, companies spend cash for growth – such as for acquisitions or research (R&D) – when confidence in the stock price and its positive reaction to such projects is high; which is to say, expending cash on growth projects is a bet on equity's ability to underpin itself.

(5) When companies hoard cash and reduce investment expenditures, this signals a relative favoring of cash over equity – in the framework described – which is a deflationary signal.

(6) When companies use very small cash allocations (relative to their aggregate cash balances or market capitalizations) to acquire entrepreneurial platforms for the technologies that these have produced, this is for the acquirer a foregone R&D expenditure in which the risk of failure has been mitigated. It signals a preference for cash preservation, lesser risk tolerance, and cautious equity perspective. This is a deflationary signal.

(7) The use of more meaningful cash amounts (relative to aggregate balances and market capitalizations) to make consolidating acquisitions, does not only signal a predisposition to expend cash in order to grow business

prospects, but also as a means to cut costs. As this is used to enhance cash flow with external assistance, as it were, it is not in itself a bullish equity signal, but is a way to acquire more cash. It is a deflationary signal.

(8) When investors favor (substantial) cash-generating properties for IPO candidacy over companies with merely solid prospects, this is also a deflationary signal as it favors a strong present cash profile over unproven future largesse. (Here and elsewhere, we are speaking in relative terms.)

Reviewing this list, many will recognize the strategic and financial patterns of behavior that have – especially in the past several years – prevailed in the digital media and information technology sectors. As already suggested, this should not be surprising for a segment that has been characterized by deflationary economies. For entrepreneurs and small businesses, there are important messages in these trends, which should be studied, because large corporations and institutional investors represent funding sources and exits. Whether these messages and other conclusions carry over to fields outside the Internet is a more complex question, but one worth investigating. For now, the principal take-away for entrepreneurs should be this:

When investors and corporations signal a relatively deflationary outlook through their actions, entrepreneurship must direct its strategies accordingly, and follow one of two paths:

Either to be a top-quality source of deferred R&D for cash-rich future buyers, or to become a cash-producing cash-rich entity that may be an attractive target for its cash (or maybe itself a buyer).

Stated otherwise, business builders should think about becoming either the outsourced R&D group, with true technological innovation, or else the money proper.

8. Of bitcoins, apps and new professions

In other news, economics remains misunderstood. Of this there are perpetual reminders. As central bankers think through the side effects of monetary medicine (they had themselves) prescribed (in the heaviest possible dosage), other theorists are honing in on a spreadsheet error. Apparently, policy decisions were predicated on a miscalculation, or a formula based on misplaced inputs, or some other circular mess, don't ask, I don't think anyone really knows, and wait till they get their hands on the poor intern. "But sir, you said…" "Never mind what I said! I say lots of things!" In this our world of macroeconomics.

With this fairly comprehensive summary by way of backdrop, the Bitcoin phenomenon is a never-ending source of fascination. To call it a bubble is erroneous, in the purest sense, because that would imply a market price far past some fundamental worth. That latter thing, however, does not technically exist. Thus, "a bubble in relation to what?" is not an easy question to answer. There are plenty of theories, some more grabbing than others (even if essentially meaningless). What the Bitcoin phenomenon has served to accomplish, however, is to draw attention to questions about value and perception, the role of central planning, the role of the market, the interrelation between information and capital, the many meanings of currency and the nature of its flows, and the complexity of this whole web of partial facts and incomplete ideas that ultimately shapes an economy.

One wonders if the Bitcoin surge, collapse, partial rebound, and subsequent fluctuations, and the series of unanswered questions that have come out of the attention all of this has garnered, have taken some toll on other markets also. Gold, for instance, that strong silent type and medium of exchange which heretofore could be relied upon for old-school concreteness and material substance, has behaved in unspeakable ways, that miners and chemists would find shocking. Maybe less so economists: Like philosophers, it takes a lot to make an economist blush, having by this time seen all sorts, explained all kinds, and built great models.

All kidding aside, these thoughts about substance versus theory and science versus economics bring to mind some of Peter Drucker's ideas about a post-capitalist era in which knowledge is the store of value and knowledge-work the basis of new professions. In modern parlance, we can think of knowledge as data, analytics, information, content, and we can think of associated professions in finance, engineering, education, healthcare, law, and other service functions built on the understanding of particular knowledge realms. The results of such knowledge and knowledge-work are, in modern parlance, *applications*.

Applications are not necessarily actions, but also tools, and in some cases directions. We tend these days to think of applications as apps, by force of habit and cultural inclination, which is a limited and narrow sense of something much broader and more complicated. By the same token, a great deal of complexity has lately been reduced to apps, and I think there is a tendency sometimes and in some professions to reduce some things to formula and menu-based selection.

While there are efficiency advantages in this approach, we have seen that models can be flawed and relying on these can be dangerous. We also now suspect that math alone isn't enough to base a currency upon. And knowledge, we sometimes find, is not where we expected to find it.

9. Gravity and grace

Sometimes it comes natural to think about spiritual subjects, including entrepreneurship and investments. And because we're all entrepreneurs and also investors, it's natural that we should think about the spirituality of Simone Weil, who suffered from insomnia and migraines in the battle trenches. The subject that I've thought about a great deal is that of weight and weightlessness. Weil wrote about the subject in a book that bears the title of this essay (in tribute), but the weight and weightlessness I am thinking about is of a different variety, sort of.

If we think about the businesses we build, or the investments we make, as summarized by the equity value that these reflect, then we can similarly consider these businesses and investments in the context of two underlying components: the asset and the optionality – as has been described and repeated in other chapters already. The asset is the core, the substance, the day-in and day-out; optionality is the unknown future, which may or may not be determined by the asset. The asset is heavy and it weighs the business down – with legacy, with definition, with obligations, with having to complete what one started and playing out a role, to say nothing of infrastructure and perhaps leverage and other things that one can actually wrap one's arms around and squeeze.

Optionality, on the other hand, is in the air. It is a set of possibilities (as opposed to the impossibilities that can also define an asset). Optionality has limits, it cannot be all possibilities because then it would be nothing at all. But it is the sum of all possible futures that a business or an investment may hold, and it is a substantial ingredient of equity value. We like to say that volatility enhances option value, and we say this because the more strongly the winds of change blow the more these toss possibilities about. Some options end up settling at great heights. Of course, when possibilities settle, this makes them no longer options but assets… which isn't a bad thing necessarily, but the weightlessness dissipates then, because with assets come responsibilities, and so on, as mentioned.

It's inevitable that potential should eventually convert to actuality (including failed actuality, if that makes sense), and that is moreover a good thing. No businesses could survive as pure possibility (although Twitter did make that last for a while, in a sense) and eventually equity value must substantiate itself with an actual underlying asset. But the dichotomy between asset and option, between weight and weightlessness, actuality and possibility, becomes conflicted in an environment of rapid evolution: One builds a business, based on a technology or market trend, and then the environment changes. The asset built may or may not be valuable after the change, and what then? At what price?

For investors, maybe this is another way of saying, know when to exit. And that's no ground-breaking revelation. For entrepreneurs, perhaps the moral of the tale is that adapting to a fast-paced and continuously changing environment should consist of balancing assets and options. Pure optionality is never a good long-term recipe in business, as stated, but neither is locking into a rigid definition, especially not nowadays. Even the biggest and most successful operations in media at the present time – Google, Apple, Facebook and Amazon – are working hard to keep their options open and not get trapped inside one sphere.

It isn't easy for such enormous asset-bases to stay nimble, and this is where the little ones have an edge. Knowing how to manage the value of weightlessness may, in the end, prove to be the equalizer, the leveler of the playing field between startups and incumbents, made possible by a unique environment of rapid change, inordinate volatility, and entrepreneurs who know how to capitalize on these things.

10. Woody's energy and distance

In the past few chapters particular attention has been paid to themes of entrepreneurship, which on reflection are probably universal. We are all entrepreneurs, though some may not realize it, and anyway it's a matter of definition. Extending the subject's scope as broadly or narrowly as one likes, the distinction still remains between the successful entrepreneurs and the less successful. (I hesitate to use this arbitrary measure, suspecting as I do that many of the truest entrepreneurs don't see themselves as successful, it being an endless task. Today's success was yesterday's failure, and tomorrow is another day.) But as arbitrary as this sort of distinction may be, it is nevertheless useful to draw it, if for no other reason than to study the method of those on one side of the line versus those on the other.

Books have been written on the subject, speeches have been given, business school programs designed and consultancies erected. It certainly isn't my belief that a little chapter in a little book can possibly capture the whole of a reality so complex, so angular, so fickle. If anything, this is thinking out loud, jotting down observations as they come to mind. In another week, or later today, other observations will follow, no doubt, and these may negate or support the going-in position, which anyway will be forgotten. And this, in part, is the point: Entrepreneurship is about results, as entertaining as the philosophy may be for a moment or two. For current purposes, the entertainment comes from Woody Allen, an entrepreneur whose success deserves to be studied.

The subject is interesting for purposes of current discussion because filmmakers – who build a new business with each new product they release – are entrepreneurs, and this particular filmmaker – who built some 40 businesses in this fashion – did so outside of the big studio system. Such stubborn independence is about as pure as entrepreneurship gets, and the subject is no less relevant than any case study out of Silicon Valley or the industrial revolution. This entrepreneur has ideas, he recruits teams to execute the same, he raises capital to fund the execution, and he sells his product much like a marketer or a founder who exits. He has been doing this for more than forty years, regularly, so I would say that is something like serial entrepreneurship with a track record.

In this case study there are two characteristics that especially caught my attention: the subject's energy, and the subject's ability to stay removed. These are mental aspects that require practice and discipline, much like an assortment of muscles in the physical sense. And the more one works out, as it were, the healthier one becomes. In the example of the filmmaker, I was struck by the steady diet of jokes that Woody Allen wrote each day – 20, 30, sometimes 40 – in his formative years, as a young columnist for the local papers. Later in life this evolved to a movie every year, an ongoing regimen, that all stems out of hundreds of seeds regularly planted – which is to say, ideas scribbled on hundreds of little papers, and stacked in a drawer for eventual review.

This mental energy, which may be a cause or an effect of regular exercise, is in some ways antithetical to another quality of the filmmaker's, which may be natural or is perhaps another trait requiring active pursuit. I am referring to a certain humbleness, a distance, an ability to see from a wide angle and thus to perceive the ultimate smallness of his work. When inviting actors and actresses to join him in a new production, he writes them personal notes to introduce himself, as if they would not know him otherwise. When the script is sent over, he tells them to feel free to make changes because individual lines are not particularly important. When he directs, he tells the actors and actresses he recruited to just do what they do best, and then he gets out of the way.

Energy and distance, focus and largesse, passion and comedy, detail and ease, remembering and forgetting: these are the contradictions that often determine success and that, in the last analysis, make entrepreneurs of us all, as has already been suggested.

11. Velocity culture

Google. Facebook. Apple. Amazon. In media and information, this is the group to watch. For now. The following perspective, from outside looking in, is not to the exclusion of others who may be as or more successful in their way.

In the respective fields and outside, through changes and fragmentation, with new entrants and incumbents on all sides, the quartet is one from which to learn. To claim that search functionality, the iPhone, commerce, the social frenzy that feeds on itself, are causes of this group's huge and growing status, would be to imply that these companies have landed into their respective places almost by accident, and this is simply not true. Their success is the result of something fundamental and no accident at all.

In each case, the organization has been able to transcend its original competitive circle and not only expand out of an original product or line, but redefine a sector and, in many cases, redefine competitors on its terms. Google stopped being just a search engine years ago. Apple could have stopped with the Mac product and chosen to carve out a comfortable niche in the education market. Facebook could have been another Friendster, and had every opportunity to be just that. But what these companies have done instead, and the way they have gone about it, is a lesson in enterprise.

"Unless you are breaking stuff you are not moving fast enough." Thus, Mr. Zuckerberg. The number of new services and features rolled out by Facebook in the past couple of years is mind-numbing. Over to Google: On certain weeks it will have introduced a new programming language, a new location based service, a new handset to compete against the best of them in wireless telecom, and maybe a new operating system for good measure. Apple, in the meantime, will be toying with yet another tablet, which may or may not threaten the Kindle and the laptop, and with improvements to its TV device that could redefine pay television in due course. Now that the company has changed the way we listen to music and the standard by which we measure the quality of telephone equipment, taking on new consumer utilities seems a natural extension. What these companies and also Amazon – books, shoes, web services, publishing – all have in common, as different as they may be in other ways, is an ingrained spirit for *velocity*, and a virtually endless energy supply.

While some other giants have either been slowed down by their bulk, or have otherwise paused in their upward trajectory to rub their eyes or high-five their comrades in disbelief at their good fortune, these four particular giants have never lost the drive to charge ahead. They seem, better than many, to have understood, that in this dynamic and volatile age even the most mature and profitable incumbent is a startup, every day.

12. Incumbency culture

I reflect back on cycles and the patterns of the start-up ecosystems. The argument is made, convincingly, that the cycle of entrepreneurship and innovation in a given geography runs its course over a 30-year stretch. During the first decade, entrepreneurs and their financial backers muddle their way through and learn lessons. During the second decade, the same group of characters (not necessarily literally) tries it a second time, having now learned from original errors, and is therefore more likely to get it right and create lasting value. In the third decade the start-up and venture capital ecosystem is fully mature, and perhaps by extension the upside opportunity diminishes.

Where Silicon Valley was twenty years ago or more, New York is now. In light of what Silicon Valley has produced in the past several decades, I surely hope that is true. I wonder, though, if the stage has really been set in New York the same way it had been set in San Francisco for the great successes that ensued.

With all things equal, but I will explain below why I do not think all things are equal, the described cyclical interpretation of history presupposes that evolution proceeds at a steady pace. As some have pointed out, however, there is an acceleration. In information technology and media and related sectors this acceleration is perhaps more noticeable than elsewhere, as more disruptive changes have occurred and newer modes introduced within a span of years, it seems, than had been done in prior tens and twenties. If one were to adjust the 30-year calculation, therefore, by this factor, then New York should have already caught up with Silicon Valley some time ago.

But this has not happened, and there may be several reasons for it. To begin with, the innovation that was occurring on the west coast in the 70s and 80s was not merely tweaking existing concepts and business models, in the same sense that New York startups are for the most part doing today. This community has tended to build on older forms, either improving the technique or extending into new markets... though not necessarily transforming these.

This really all speaks to another major difference between eastern and western environments. In the west the strategic foundation consists of Google, Facebook, Amazon, and Apple – companies that were upstarts not long ago and that continue to innovate to this day. In New York, by contrast, the strategic community includes organizations that have in some cases been in existence for more than a century, and which have dominated their respective fields for the better part of that time. Such outfits are less likely than others to push for change, but rather defend a fenced-off area. This is a dominant gene, as it were, in the environment, which creates ripples and effects on the culture and the system.

It has been argued by some that the present-time industrial revolution is based on data, much like previous revolutions were based on factories and assembly lines and corporations. If that is true, and I think it is, this time around the powerful incumbents are nimble and fast and energetic. Perhaps this is in reflection of an underlying asset – information – that is itself light and malleable. Or maybe the light malleability creates threats to the incumbency that, in another era, was shielded by the barriers of heavy substances and systems.

The modern enterprise – its investors and its labor – are being trained in a school that is really still building its curriculum ad hoc. Our incumbency is actually no incumbency at all. Some see that.

The Digitized Character & Reorientation

1. The grandeur of analog

There is a scene in the coming-of-age movie, *Almost Famous*, in which the 11-year old boy discovers his older sister's record collection. As he feels his way through the large covers, pausing at times to move his hand across the cover art, we can almost sense the director's tenderness thinking back, and the boy's wonderment, about the mystery that lies inside the sleeves. That sense of anticipation, the discovery, flipping through the now-classic albums and those big square images, is brought to a climax when the needle of a plastic turntable arm drops on the vinyl – thump – and the crackling of dust and static serves as a second-long intro to the opening riffs of *Tommy*.

Some of us who are old enough to remember the sensation may see the present-day parallel as a very thin shadow of it – an online sample, the click of a mouse, a Pandora suggestion, or in a best case the purchase of a tiny CD to hold, though probably not in any store where at the cash register some dude who has heard all the records is prone to pass judgment. You can still find a few such stores in the Village, but for the most part the richness and texture of the analog experience is gone. At least in music.

These observations are not merely nostalgic, although undoubtedly there is that, or meant to condescend on the new modes of entertainment consumption – which, despite the nostalgia and musings, offer convenience and excitement, discovery tools and social interaction. Nevertheless, if one web music machine after another has been shut down, restructured, or sold for nothing, we have to ask ourselves why this is. There might be more to the answer than merely "iTunes."

So, I am hereby wondering if the answer lies in the contrast between the album experience (illustrated, admittedly, with some romance, above), and the more purely utilitarian and way more rapid digital experience today. Perhaps the very nostalgia contains answers – or at least poses a question or two – about an industry that has struggled to maintain its economic and cultural prominence of late.

It has been well documented that the music-revenue opportunity of both record labels and artists has declined, and in many cases drastically. There have been a variety of reasons presented for this decline, from piracy to fragmentation to alternative free content... and on a certain level all of these explanations really speak to the same issue: a consumer experience that has been cheapened.

The album art and liner notes on CDs are small and negligible, and in the case of downloads almost completely absent. The sound quality in low bit-rate digital recordings is poor in comparison to analog vinyl. Songs that would have been "out-takes" in the 8-10 album-track era now make up tracks number 9 or 10 through 15, in the much greater memory bank of a CD. And the number of artists who have found an outlet on the web, almost impossible to keep up with, means that fewer and fewer make it "big." The glue, in other words, that is a large fan base and community is spread out more thinly, and dissolved.

There will be solutions in the sector, and new products will spring up. There will be new stars, such as Spotify – and as was already mentioned in another chapter, the medium *is* the new star, after all – and new styles, which will give rise to new tastes and new enthusiasm. New forms of grandeur will emerge, that will make us forget the old.

In the here and now, however, and with the experience of music behind us, one can't help but see the trends and technologies popping up in all forms of media and entertainment and information – online video, for example, and eBooks, and photo sharing, and native advertising, and the networks and exchanges that place impressions and make predictions and fight for that incremental basis point of click-through – one looks at all of this and wonders… Are these modes taking both the economic opportunity and the consumer experience down the same path? And is there a parallel, or indeed a direct connection, between the value of technology and the depth of its human aspect, on some level? Maybe on several.

2. The paid and thinning content

The New York author, David Markson, in later years wearied of long paragraphs and grew to mistrust narrative. He wrote his later "novels" as a series of blurbs. These blurbs rarely exceed a couple of short lines and are assembled in seemingly random order. Leafing through one of these books the other day, I had a bit of fun imagining the narrative as an extended Twitter feed. If only! One doesn't often come across such exquisite messaging – wherein even the most mundane anecdotage is elegant, thought provoking, ironic – not even from marketers. One may think of these Markson novels as professionally crafted and premium-priced tweets, for which we should be thrilled to pay.

This led me to consider – and a glance through my actual Twitter stream prodded me in these musings – the misfortune we would suffer if professionally crafted content were to be wholly displaced by amateur, or worse, machine-generated product. For some time, the open and fragmented Internet, the free web, which isn't actually free but advertising based on one hand, and data frenzied on the other, has taken us in that direction. Although we are not all the way there, yet, and although there is still plenty of premium quality in the marketplace, the proportions are skewing, and the economics are increasingly challenged.

So what, you may ask, does this have to do with the iPad? The answer is, a lot. We have all heard the case for the open web, or if any of you have not, take a moment to visit the Google homepage, type in a term, any term, even gibberish, and you'll be flooded with ideas. With the iPad, on the other hand, and for that matter all Apple products, openness is not the priority but design and quality control are. In the open web, even I can have a platform. The iPad, thus, has its appeal.

If it is true, as some believe, that the iPad is becoming the home-entertainment unit, through which we access books, magazines, movies and other videos, games, music, and even control our television sets remotely, this could go a long way to check the content value free-fall. This might give professional creators a mass-market and unified platform through which to distribute their wares presentably, with less clutter, and for payment received.

If premium content, in the long term, has any chance at all against the onslaught of free noise and fragmentation, then it might take a well-designed and hugely popular consumer distribution alternative to save it through its packaging. In this essay, the case of the iPad per se is meant to be more symbolic than actual. As Markson's book reminded me, we should perhaps be more wary than we are about a future dominated by amateur production. (There was, until recently, a side-table towards the back of the main aisle at the Strand Bookstore on Broadway and 12th Street, on which stacks of David Markson novels were offered at a discount.)

3. The possibility of islands

The French author, Michel Houellebecq, published a novel some years ago – at a time when Facebook had not been the international sensation it has become, when Twitter did not exist, and when the social web was still new enough and at the same time intriguing enough to loom with mystery and possibilities – and in this novel, *The Possibility of an Island*, a future society is explored in which generations of clones live their lives in complete individual isolation, communicating with each other from stationary and remote locations through computers. All human interaction, in this fictional future, occurs digitally, and I confess that I did not find the scenario in the least bit implausible, or even particularly ominous or futuristic. I have ever since kept a sort of watch, out of the corner of my eye, for trends in media that would take us further and further in the direction described. With this by way of background, I really like what the location-based mobile services, such as Foursquare and others, are doing.

What I like about the Foursquare platform, what I find sort of touching, is the presentation of physical locations, with physical addresses – diners, office buildings, drugstores, museums, the couch in somebody's living room, it doesn't matter – in a way that on one level resembles web browsing, and the premise of a mobile service that encourages its users to be, as much as possible, outside and in the world.

Now, twenty years ago, Foursquare would have been pointless. "Just go outside," we would have argued, why do you need to "have an app for that?" But we've changed, haven't we? We are the social generation now in the Facebook sense, with apps for everything, and in this context Foursquare not only makes sense but is a welcome addition. Each time we check into a locale, our visit is catalogued, much like an online browsing history is a catalogue of all the virtual places we visit. And when we do this checking in we leave a print, we leave our mark on the establishment and we leave a note in our personal file where moments and travels are recorded. One day we may look back... we'll find most of the places gone, and we'll remember.

The collective memory is really the subject of what is now called "big data," and on a smaller individual level the little data is our own personal memoir. Where big data is used to make predictions and study large-scale activity, the little data serves its purpose as well.

It is said that the Foursquare platform is addictive for some, and since I have only been on it sporadically I can't clinically vouch. I kind of hope that it is, and if you've read Houellebecq you will understand why I say this. The virtualization and mechanization, the digitization and structure of a so-called mobile existence is already upon us and there isn't any turning back; perhaps it's useful, even wholesome, to put it to more deeply human use.

4. Social media and organized self-expression

Is your status married or single? In love is not an option, and engaged doesn't count: Make your selection. Is your profession finance/accounting or management/leadership? If some of each, you better think fast. Do your musical preferences run to rock/pop or jazz/blues? Forget nuance, just check the box and move on, your best guess is close enough.

That these and many other categories are inappropriate, incomplete, or misplaced, is the price we pay for being "connected" and "informed." You can't have millions of individuals self-expressing all at once without some convenient compromise for purposes of data aggregation and targeted advertising. You can't have billions of messages flow through the system during a given period and explain yourself in more than 140 characters (counting spaces and punctuation).

This brings to mind bits of Huxley's *Brave New World Revisited*, in which the author reviews the far-out and futuristic prophesies of his youthful novel, noticing that some are already well ahead of schedule. Among these, "Over-Organization" resulting from over-population. The notion of a crowd does not have to be taken literally: One billion on Facebook, hundreds of millions using Twitter, and whatever the latest subscriber count of LinkedIn, these are all an acceptable proxy.

And I am also reminded of Foucault's *The Order of Things*, in which the artificiality of classification in our civilization is introduced as follows, (actually, quoting Borges, quoting a certain Chinese encyclopedia, that does not exist):

"Animals are divided into: (a) belonging to the Emperor, (b) embalmed, (c) tame, (d) sucking pigs, (e) sirens, (f) fabulous, (g) stray dogs, (h) included in the present classification, (i) frenzied, (j) innumerable, (k) drawn with a very fine camelhair brush, (l) et cetera, (m) having just broken the water pitcher, (n) that from a long way off look like flies."

So, are you in finance/accounting or do you like jazz/blues music?

Foucault's theories, kidding aside, have to do with the related forces of power and freedom, and the individual's place that lies in balance. Taken in this context, it is probably not too far a stretch to say that the artificial limitations of social media are an exercise of power on the individual, whose freedom of self-expression is constrained by it.

Zadie Smith once published an article in *The New York Review of Books*, which was part movie review (of *The Social Network*) and part analysis of the Facebook effect on our generations. One of the more interesting observations she makes is that, over time, Facebook users will tend –

rather than to really express themselves – to conform to the classification that the social network bestows upon them, (based on, among other things, their consumption habits.)

Perhaps the next breakthrough in mass communication, and social media in particular, will be a system that liberates users from such boundaries. Perhaps the next phase of social media will be a theater of the absurd, in which we can truly be ourselves.

Until then, the consumers of the data we generate through our interactions will have to be mindful: The analytic result and the predicted patterns are only as useful as the inputs are true.

5. The author's voice

I am thinking about nuance, about the space between the digits. If 1s and 0s make up our communication systems, I am thinking about the messages that get lost. It's a complex subject, extending beyond the isolated confines of programming. The binary simplicity of code has its parallels in other modern systems and perceptions, and maybe a program can solve the circular causality.

Take, for instance, the term *social graph*, used to describe the totality of our interactions. Take *LOL*, an expression of humorous appreciation. Take big data, a way of collecting information about whole groups of individuals. Or take even high-frequency trading, the dominant driver of capital markets volume, often associated with programmed interpretation of news headlines. These are examples of depth reduced by formula, color translated by algorithm, even if only as a form of expression.

This reduction is a necessary step in technological evolution, which in the last century (and the last decade even), has made strides. But there is a risk, I think, in premature celebration and basking in the glow of what is still an intermediate step. If our digital solutions end here, if our communication mechanisms stop at the current 1s and 0s and simplistic LOLs, this will have been an underachievement.

The next goal, at least to my way of thinking, should be to capture the space between the digits, the nuance; and when this occurs – when the grandeur of analog is recaptured by digital – the truer potential of technology should be one step closer to realization. (Artificial intelligence, as a general field, is possibly the forefront in this effort, and it is indeed a very large field and work-in-progress. Siri herself would confess to that, in her sarcastic monotone.)

To elaborate on the idea, we sample three Bob Dylan recordings of the same one song, *Idiot Wind*. Each is the same melody, with more or less the same lyrics, telling the same story ("Someone's got it in for me, they're printing stories in the press…") in the same key with the same chords. And yet, each is an entirely different story because the author's voice is different in each of them. There is the *Blood on the Tracks* official-release version, marked by anger, defiance, and occasional irony; there is the outtake in the *Bootleg Series*, on which the voice is toned down and the song becomes a melancholy, often heart-wrenching, reflection; and there is the live rendition on *Hard Rain*, care-free, liberated, almost jubilant. The same song, three different songs… and what galaxies of meaning there must surely be in every trifle of an LOL.

The point here, again, is not to pick on text messaging or emoticons or social graphs and big data and high-frequency trading, but to illustrate the diminishing and constraining quality of these methods that underlie much of our communication and digital technology. Nor is the point to pick on the technology that has produced advances in science, economies, living conditions. The commentary, rather, is in relation to the distance that must still be traveled before we can rest (if even then). And on some level, I suppose, it's also a statement that we shouldn't settle, content to reside in some demographic definition, some trading algorithm, some graph. These are all intermediate stages towards a goal, means to other means to others, and so on, rather than a discrete conclusion.

The digital technology that has dominated our connected systems is often like song lyrics read in the manner of text, in isolation, without melody, tonality, and the singer's interpretation. From the perspective of the audience, these are like boos or cheers, 1s and 0s, the only possible reaction.

6. The brevity of our perspectives

The question was posed, as questions so often are, on Twitter. To paraphrase: How can a budget-cut grow GDP and reduce unemployment? The reference was to the debt deal struck that same day in Washington, and the question was asked sort of rhetorically, I believe, although with these blurbs there is always plausible denial.

I wouldn't have given the tweet a second thought, had it not originated from a technology investor of some stature. And although I don't often converse on Twitter, it being a newswire for me rather than conversation mechanism, I was tempted to join the discussion. But the challenge proved too much. How does one reduce the world's biggest economy to 140 characters? How does one reduce any economic idea to 140 characters? I gave up... whatever... soon distracted by some other snippet.

Maybe we do too much conversing about complicated subjects in simple ways, and maybe this is something we should monitor more somberly. Have we been programmed to limit our expression to blurbs? I hope not, but – to use the referenced tweet as an example – the asker of the question posed it on Twitter and expected replies on the same medium. The format, incidentally, was also proposed by the powers that be as the way to contact one's congressional representative with politico-economic feedback.

Among the thousands of perspectives shared in 140 characters or less that day, one caught my attention and captured the essence of the moment. It was from one concerned constituent to a senator: "Dude compromise man!!!"

Perfect. Debate over, and with characters to spare.

7. The big frontier in the space between the bits

There isn't any noise, there is only signal. We think of the two as separate and contrasting because we seek simple solutions to complex problems. We look for straight answers to questions that are often nuanced, and we try to match simple sets of data to complicated subjects. Or rather, we try to simplify the clues that complex data provide. We seek to eliminate noise from signal presupposing that the question is correct and that there is only one correct answer to it. Sometimes this is the case, but not always. And sometimes noise is actually signal, only for a different question.

I've been reading Nate Silver. *The Signal and the Noise* has been a true pleasure: thought provoking, interesting, and, as importantly, really well written. I find it refreshing that a statistician with well documented credentials has written a book to remind us about inaccuracy, about chaos and dynamism, degrees and relativity, greater or lesser probabilities as opposed to absolutes and binary yes-no extremes. There is something like awe, or at least a becoming humility, recognizing the limitations of quantitative data in the context of human and natural experience that is far more frequently qualitative.

I am reminded, reading the case studies and commentary in this book, about a chasm I sometimes detect that may be analogous to digital versus analog communication. On one hand there are systems and resulting behavior based on a rigid algorithmic approach, limited by charts and boxes and bits and formula, and on the other hand there is nature. There is the music download at 160 kbps, and there is the live performance. There is the 140-character micro-message, and there is actual conversation. But beyond such commonplace samples it's possible to make the point more meaningful with illustrations from financial markets.

Algorithmic trading versus fundamental analysis is a literal example, but although extreme it is inherently really a question of degree. The application of inflexible formula and a superficial approach is on some level the same when, say, a startup with a necessarily formulaic profile is funded through standardized terms, and is expected to raise additional capital within a standard timeframe and to "exit" in a standard manner after that. Consider all of the formulaic points at which perfectly legitimate businesses would fail to fit the equation. Consider this especially in an IPO environment welcoming only to specific types that can satisfy minimum volume requirements (sufficient to keep algorithmic trade active).

Just as predictive analysis through the computerized processing of enormous amounts of data is efficient on one level but highly inefficient on another – as described by Silver in his book – and just as conversing through tweets is efficient at scale but also limiting individually, so also the financial markets illustrated carry their own set of inefficiencies, even as more businesses of bigger magnitude and scope are funded. The inefficiency in this case has something to do with valuation gaps, which the markets tend to correct and fill out in due course. More fundamentally, however, there is inefficiency in the funding mechanism itself and what this does to force businesses to conform to artifice, even if nature would dictate otherwise.

The big opportunity, and what may prove to be the next large frontier, will be for business builders, financiers, and other innovators to recapture the analog experience in a digital environment. The idea has been broached here already.

8. An app for intuition

Patterns and pattern recognition are topical subjects when machines learn and algorithms predict. When push comes to shove, the method and very purpose of computing is to uncover and build upon patterns. In comparisons that are drawn by the purists, the classicists, between the human mind and the mechanical device, the argument is always made about nuances and subtleties that computers can't detect. In sports, for instance, there is a player's "heart" and team "chemistry" and a batter's "trouble with the curve," and such things that are beyond data sampling.

Perhaps. But more truly the limitations of modern computing and data science are a matter of degree and will likely diminish as technology evolves. Which is to say, it isn't necessarily the technique, it isn't necessarily a fault of logic, that limits computational possibilities, but rather the lines of code – a state that will catch up. A matter of time really, and there is plenty of that. At some point, arguably, intuition is bound to become computable as well, or, in modern parlance, there will be an app for that.

At least this is what my intuition tells me, and intuition is often wrong. But this isn't about predictions, which are hard, very hard, (thankfully). This is about pattern recognition, or taking note of the actual. One pattern that is discernible to some has been a declining interest in arts and humanities in favor of more technical subjects at higher-level educational institutions. While this is understandable from an economic perspective, at least in so far as the present economic state is concerned, it may also be shortsighted and signify a misunderstanding of technology – a field at the service of mankind, rather than vice versa – unless humanities and the arts become marginalized and drowned out in formulaic patter of technical innovation.

A second pattern, in ways overarching, is an increasing research emphasis on the human brain – a relatively uncharted frontier. Hundreds of thousands of years in the making, give or take, the modern brain is about as complex a mechanism as any quantum computer. And we've taken this mobile device for granted: about the size of an iPad Mini but more like a small toaster, we bring it with us everywhere.

While there are medical reasons to be excited about the increased research focus, there should also be reasons of computer science. Understanding the architecture and synapses of this ancient mechanism (with intuition functionality fully integrated) might enable us to emulate certain design features, improve on some existing ones, and understand limitations and possibilities in ways we may not understand today.

For instance, a recent study of music and the brain, or more precisely the effect of the former upon the latter, suggests an interesting aspect of music appreciation: "Each act of listening to music may be thought of as both recapitulating the past and predicting the future. When we listen to music, these brain networks actively create expectations based on our stored knowledge."

Who would have thought that one of the inherent joys of music lies in pattern recognition and predictive analytics? Among the myriad associations between humanities, art and the sciences, who would heretofore have made this particular connection?

9. Truth as technology's lasting value

A fellow once wrote this: "We are what we pretend to be, so we must be careful about what we pretend to be." He was a clever fellow, prolific, argumentative, a blogger in his way, (but who isn't?). He died, alas, before this medium really took off, and anyway, he was probably more of the typewriter variety. So it goes. The cited wisdom could be applied to many a context, some of which may have been imagined by the author, but for some reason it currently makes me think of the information sector, which nowadays comprises many aspects, as discussed, (and more below).

I am thinking that media, as a general category of industry, is uniquely positioned to report upon and conduct its own assessment. A sector populated (and even defined) by carriers of the message – bloggers, analysts, researchers, marketers, advertisers, publicists, podcasters, broadcasters, journalists, tweeters – can shape the message and define itself with few checks and balances. Any such controls would necessarily also come from within, from other carriers of the message. The situation is a little bit analogous to, for instance, Michael Jordan calling his own fouls. (Some secretly suspected that this happened all the time.) So too with media: A sector that gets to call its own game. What luck.

But not really. One could argue, in fact, that this is a misfortune. To illustrate, let's take a scenario of a different type from that of an arbitrary calling of shots. Take for example, software code. Putting aside qualitative aspects like programming efficiency and elegance, in a very fundamental way the code either works or doesn't. This is a binary condition that cuts to the truth of the case very precisely, so that a syntax error could throw the whole thing off. In one way of looking at it, and as painful as such a process may appear, this binary precision is its very beauty and is the trait that gives it lasting value. On the other hand, when one gets to define one's own reality freely, that is where true anxiety lies. (The concept of anxiety and freedom is not new, "we are what we pretend to be, so we must be careful about what we pretend to be.")

Now, media is a vast universe and getting vaster. Not only is this true in the sense of new technologies and modes that have entered the domain and continue to enter – mobility, interactivity, data and its assortment of branches, security, artificial intelligence, and others – but also in terms of enriched applications. As has been contemplated in previous chapters, the segment also comprises capital markets – perhaps this was always so (the example one likes to use is Bloomberg, media or financial technology company?), but now maybe more obviously than ever – and this is where the notion of self-reporting takes on a more than philosophical turn.

The circularity is wonderful, and so is the snowball effect that sometimes perpetuates. In certain instances the snowball becomes a bubble that pops, and sometimes it grows like any rolling snowball. Sometimes, as well, observers get swept up by the rolling mass and cycle through it actively, perpetuating whatever fashion the sector's trend-setters-cum-trend-reporters lead. When in rare instances an industry observer is able to step out of the cycle and look upon the scene with a fresh and distant perspective – such as, for example, Peter Thiel in his famous lecture series at Stanford – the experience is refreshing to the point of being almost hypnotic. (Perhaps this is so because of the nearly mathematical logic and clarity of the class, and the feeling one gets that maybe he isn't even "talking his book.")

But precisely because of expediency and improved efficiencies enabled by the technologies now residing in the media domain, we should not have to rely on rare instances of individual vision. In other words, the opportunity exists, in capital markets and in media – which have become increasingly synonymous – for information flow to be optimized, scrubbed clean, and made useful. That, ultimately, will be the dominant and lasting value-proposition of our evolving field, and it's the direction in which the sector is heading.

Afterword

1.

Pattern recognition, data visualization, information processing are the recounting of stories. Facebook timelines, Twitter streams, LinkedIn updates, Google searches and results, much like reality TV, are stories, too. Stock charts and analyses, financial ratios and credit ratings, research reports, are variations, commentaries, stories about stories, and so on. Journalistic content and entertainment product, often interchangeable, are stories unabashedly, if previously listed examples are maybe less self-aware. When an entrepreneur pitches a venture capitalist, a story is told much like a filmmaker pitching a studio chief. In turn, investors tell stories to explain the risk that's taken.

When we speak about a new era of information, a new economy based on information flow and connectivity, we are speaking about a world of stories. The world was always one of stories to some degree, but this was more obviously contained in myth, philosophy, politics, religion, or art. It may be that these realms have expanded, or it may be that new fields have been introduced into the fray as a result of digital technology and global interconnection. More likely, things are the same as always, but we now recognize the stories more clearly as a part of our practical – not only spiritual – existence... which are anyway interlinked.

In the world of investments and finance there have been notable examples in recent times of leadership figures (such as Michael Moritz or Steven Rattner) that came out of journalism rather than what may be considered more conventional breeding grounds. This is not a cause but a result of the environment described. And when we think of Steve Jobs, recognized as a great – maybe the greatest – entrepreneur of the information age, we think of a visionary and communicator. Steve Jobs was, in short, a great storyteller. Stories do not have to be fibs, although they sometimes are, but rather messages that are unified and whole, and it helps a good deal if the message is also interesting.

Theorists of the traditional variety have liked to speculate about the vague distinction between storyteller, story, and audience, and in our age of convergence this could well be another manifestation. In an era in which information and its flow are the gravitational center, the story and the storyteller are taking on a central significance. In our time, the narrative should (and probably will) come to be seen as partner (in some cases even the lead) in a complex alliance with technology on the same side. We will (and probably should) see the stories that emerge as a form of innovation also, and this idea was never far from mind as I was jotting down my notes and discourses.

2.

Some things are probably random, and some things probably not. Probability and randomness have been financial market staples that at least one student of the trade has made a centerpiece of research and commentary. As randomness is truly a matter of degree, so probability tends to govern outcomes in many realms, not only markets. Statisticians are trained to accept this natural state, some other theorists are less inclined.

With hindsight events are usually explicable – by historians, economists, social scientists, psychologists, philosophers, and many spectator sports aficionados – even if explanations are disputed. Prediction, on the other hand, is far more difficult. Or more precisely, impossible; that is, true, confident, prediction. The number of variables that shape outcomes, directly, indirectly, and in combination, is virtually countless. Because not all of these are equally important, probability makes for complex computation.

Data science is an art in which science happens to be an instrument. Some algorithmic tools are more effective than others, but not consistently so in any circumstance. Predictive analytics in advertising, recommendation engines in commerce, trading systems and credit scoring in finance, are all tools, usually meant to be taken under advisement and heavily footnoted. The same is true in business building according to at least one builder who would know, where formulaic instruction is generously tossed around but where good fortune in the face of improbable outcome helps.

This doesn't mean that planning, strategy, and most importantly vision, should be dismissed to a toss of the dice. Nor that execution and hustle are interchangeable with luck. At least not always, and in the realm of probability these elements combine to enhance likelihoods… but… But… nevertheless.

Vision, hard work, good chemistry, even funding, are not enough. Because there is competition, and there are market forces, and changes in both, usually unforeseeable, even if explainable in retrospect. And there's that butterfly that flaps its wings in Tokyo to cause a cloud to gather down in the Sahara next year.

These things are known, or at least suspected, and accordingly stockbrokers and venture capitalists emphasize portfolio diversification. Also, it is by law required to make clear that past performance is not an indication of future results. More correctly, however, the regulatory proviso should state that past performance is always predictive of future results, but most of the time we look to the wrong past, or in the wrong way.

3.

The answers are findable, we stumble upon them at times by accident, and when we do, we often don't know it. The other instances, which are rare, are called inspiration.

Here are a handful of favored resources, which are a reading list as well as thank you note to some great storytellers, where I find inspiration. Many of them have been cited, not all have been named. But they and some others were present in these pages all the while:

P.Drucker, N.N.Taleb, C.Christensen, B.Mandelbrot, J.Lanier, M.Foucault, L.Wittgenstein, J-L.Borges, A.Huxley, R.Musil, F.Kafka, A.Rimbaud, W.Burroughs, P.K.Dick, E.Canetti, H.Arendt, S.Weill, A.Schopenhauer, N.Machiavelli, M.Aurelius, *Plato's Republic*, *The Book of Ecclesiastes*, the city of New York, F.Wilson, O.Malik and the prolific bloggers, whose output has been my daily study guide.

4.

"Well… if I feel like my song is sung, I don't care… if it's short… And I feel like my song is sung." Thus, Johnny Cash to his producer, Rick Rubin, who was joined in laughter by his entourage of recording engineers behind the glass, at the end of a 2-minute take of what should have been, in Mr. Rubin's opinion, a longer rendition of "You Are My Sunshine," a song we all know.

Some of the fragments that preceded here were short, and some could probably have been shorter. Some might have seemed disjointed and others tracked after one another in sequence. The picture, I think, is what matters, and I feel like my song is sung. More or less.

About the author

Dan Ramsden has been active in finance, strategy, and business building for more than two decades. He has specialized in media and its related technologies and services for most of that time. Ramsden has been principal and advisor, in corporate, institutional and entrepreneurial settings, and has participated in the formation and growth of startups as well as the consummation of equity, debt, and M&A transactions, public and private.

Ramsden's career began in 1987, a year in which the Black Monday crash of October served as his welcome to the scene, and he has witnessed the transition of traditional to new media, wireline to mobile, decentralized applications to the cloud, and the influence of social media and data on all segments. His experience has taught him some fundamental precepts, one of which is this: Everything changes, many things relate, and some things repeat. Knowing which of these things is which and how to navigate the dynamism and unity is the critical and ongoing challenge in technology as well as markets, which are connected.

Ramsden earned his B.A. in English Literature from Cornell University, where he also picked up on Economics, Statistics, and Computer Science. He earned his M.B.A. from Fordham University, where Accounting and Finance rounded out his academic pursuits. The rigor of study intensified greatly when formal schooling ended.

Ramsden runs a private merchant banking firm, CoRise, which he founded as a platform to participate in the evolution of information technology and its connected systems.

About the author

Dan Ramsden has been active in finance, strategy and business, building for more than two decades. He has specialized in media and financial technologies, and serving most of that time. For which he has been principal and advisor in corporate institutions and entrepreneurial ventures, and has participated in the formation of several of them, as well as the combination of a number, and numerous acquisitions.